FEEDING
the
HEART

Copyright © 2015 The Center for Discovery

Published by The Center for Discovery, Inc.
P.O. Box 840, Harris, New York 12742-0840

Department of Nourishment Arts is a registered trademark of The Center for Discovery
DNA is a registered trademark of The Center for Discovery
Food is Medicine is a registered trademark of The Center for Discovery
Seed to Belly is a registered trademark of The Center for Discovery

ISBN 978-0-9963710-0-1

For information about special sales and premium purchases,
please contact Richard Humleker, The Center for Discovery at 845-707-8506

Editor: Eileen Daspin
Design: Mister Dizney

Manufactured in China

FEEDING

the

HEART

Recipes, flavors and the
Seed to Belly philosophy
of the Department
of Nourishment Arts

THE CENTER FOR DISCOVERY

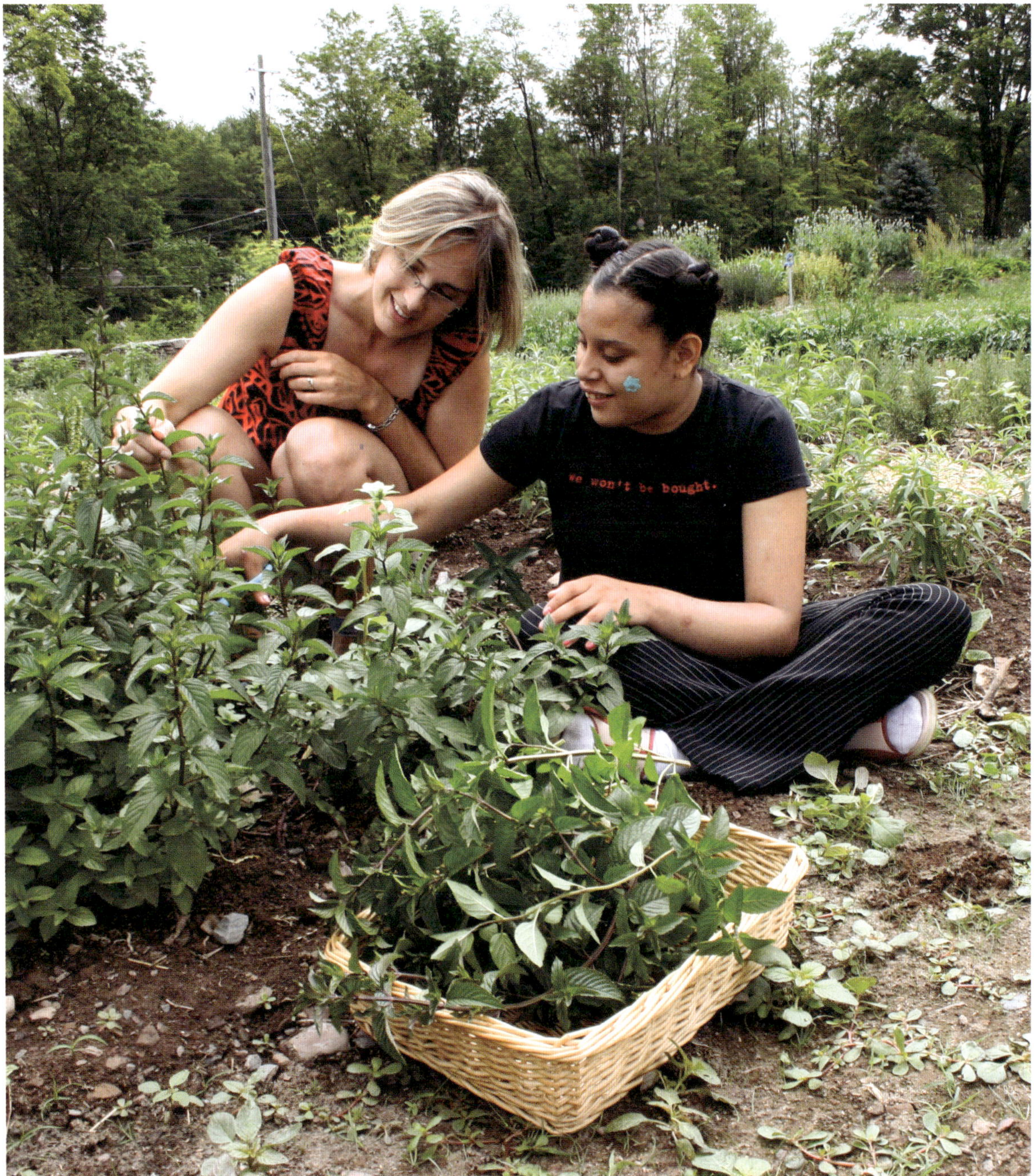
we won't be bought.

Welcome to
The Center for Discovery

Tucked away in the foothills of the Catskill Mountains is a very special place: The Center for Discovery, an oasis for children and adults with complex disabilities, medical frailties and autism spectrum disorders. A leader in its field, this unique facility manages the health, education and welfare of some 350 pediatric and adult residents, as well as more than 100 day students from outside The Center.

The program is holistic, integrating therapies, learning, nature and the arts so that residents and day students can see themselves as part of a larger world connected not only to the people around them but also the land, the animals and plants, to culture, music, books and sports. Residents and day students participate in activities you find in towns everywhere. They go to school, attend concerts, take ski trips, hike, pick apples, put on plays, swim, dance and more.

In this environment people flourish, experiencing accomplishment and developing a greater sense of independence. The Center's community includes a staff of 1,500: There are physicians and nurses, nutritionists and farmers and teachers and therapists. Residents live together in small homes and take on a variety of responsibilities. Some train and work on Thanksgiving Farm, a cluster of farms owned by The Center that provide much of the food consumed on campus. Ability is the focus here, disability a mere reminder that some people may need to do things a bit differently.

The Center's model emphasizes maintaining and promoting health through optimal food, daily exercise, exposure to green space, sound sleep and restoration of the body's natural rhythms. Staff works constantly to improve the medical and behavioral status of those in the community and collaborates with academics and clinicians across the country to do so. In addition, The Center conducts original research into how to enrich approaches to care to benefit children and families whose lives are impacted by significant disabilities.

To visit The Center is to understand the important work it does and the high standard it is setting. Patrick Dollard, The Center's CEO and president, likes to say, "If you live long enough, you join our club." By that he means that each of us will one day find ourselves in need of help. As the population ages, The Center's work will apply not only to those with complex disabilities and medical frailties, but to every human being. The philosophy here is that each person deserves humane and informed care.

Come see these principles in action as embodied by the Department of Nourishment Arts, our unique team of chefs, nutritionists and farmers who deliver daily on our core belief that Food is Medicine. Here is the story of *Feeding the Heart*.

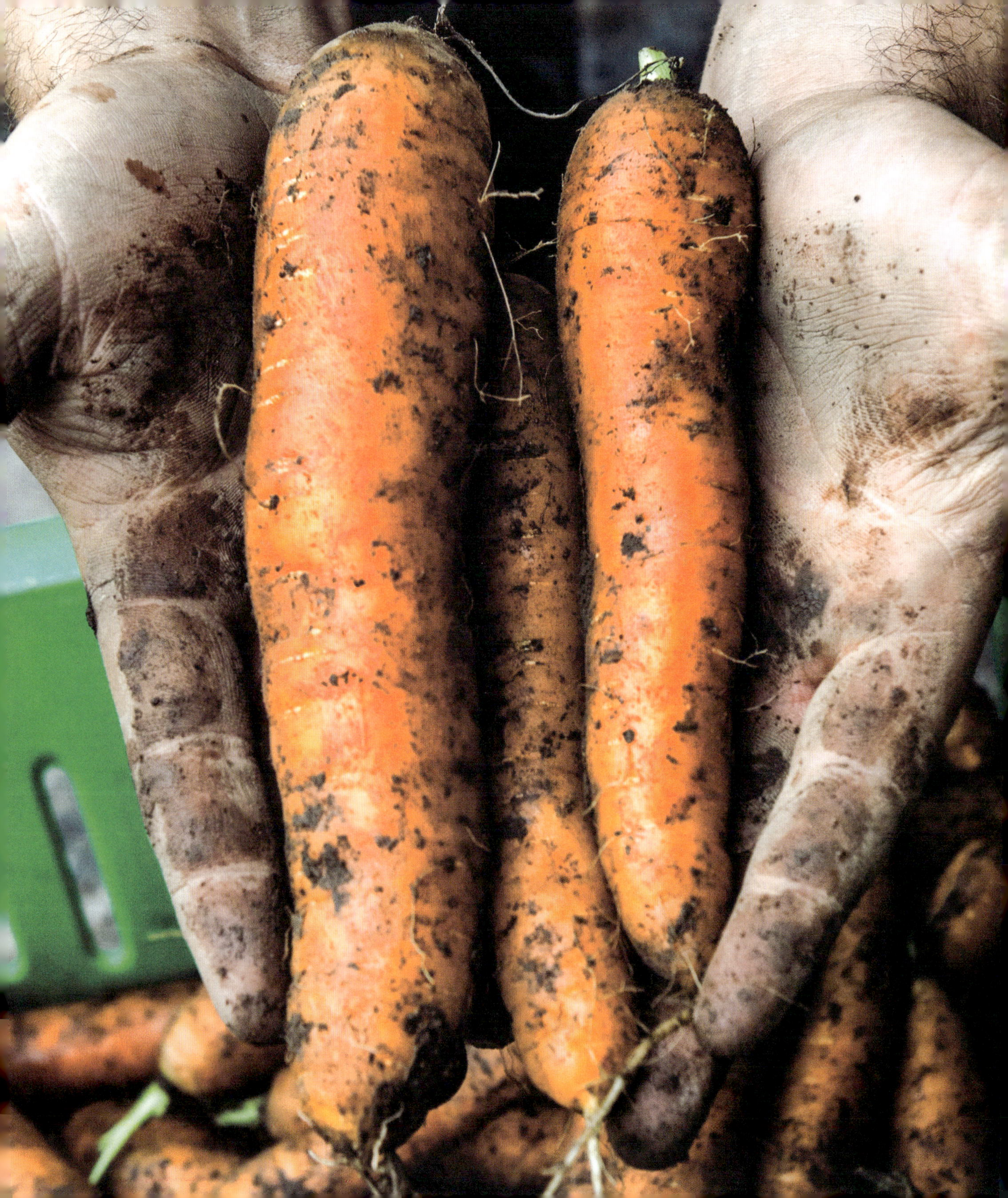

CHAPTER ONE

DNA: The Art of Nourishing

To nourish.

It is an act that defines caregiving. To nourish is to provide the nurturing essential to life. To nourish is to foster growth and strength. Nourishment is at the core of every activity at The Center for Discovery, a residential, educational, farming and medical facility in upstate New York that serves children and adults with complex disabilities and medical frailties, including autism spectrum disorders. It is a deeply felt impulse that shapes not only the people who live and work at The Center but also the animals they care for, the land they cultivate, and, rippling outward, the surrounding neighbors in Sullivan County.

At its most basic, nourishment is the food that sustains life. On campus, this work starts with the Department of Nourishment Arts, or DNA, a group of chefs, nutritionists and farmers who collaborate to optimize food and nutrition in innovative ways. The team supports The Center's fundamental belief that Food is Medicine and its efforts mirror this holistic philosophy, linking eating to therapy, farming to learning, and establishing food as the basis for health.

DNA's commitment literally starts with the seeds planted in the fields and ends with the full belly of a satisfied guest—DNA calls this cycle Seed to Belly. For the DNA team, nurturing means training and educating residents through farming. It means that the food served to all is safe, nutritious, delicious and humanely produced. It means that staff members are encouraged to improve their knowledge and sharpen their cooking skills. On The Center's campus, DNA represents the well-being that comes from connecting to food, to people, to cooking, and to the satisfaction that accompanies nurturing others.

"Traditionally, in a restaurant the goal is to make beautiful food that tastes good. At The Center we do the opposite," says Cesare Casella, chief of DNA and a chef who has owned and run many restaurants in Italy and New York City. "We

The Conversation

Members of The Center for Discovery community share their thoughts on connections; safe, delicious, nutritious food; and the rewards of their work. P. 12

The Da Vinci Master Chefs

In this restaurant-inspired training program, some of New York's best known chefs conduct seminars for DNA staff. P. 17

"We start
with great
nutrition
and make
the food taste
better. Then
it's really
beautiful."

start with great nutrition and make the food taste better. Then it's really beautiful."

This commitment to optimizing food has taken off under Chef Casella's direction at DNA. In recent years, for example, The Center has expanded its relationships with the professional restaurant community in an effort to ensure that its residential chefs have the best culinary training possible. DNA has brought in industry leaders to conduct seminars for these chefs on such topics as knife skills and perfectly cooked pasta. Some of New York City's best-known restaurant stars, from Mark Ladner of Del Posto to Bill Telepan of Telepan, have taught alongside nutritionist Jennifer Franck, assistant chief of DNA, and Peggy Parten, its executive chef and culinary director.

The professional training has benefited both The Center's staff and the residents, says Chef Casella, who created the program, called the DaVinci Master Chefs. "The staff is excited to get to meet famous chefs, to know the techniques they use and the way they share their knowledge," he says, adding that the enthusiasm translates into what is served each day in the residences. "The chefs are the ones with the most direct contact with the residents," says

Chef Casella. "The more enthusiasm they have, the more creative they get."

What's more, the success of the DaVinci Master Chef program has sparked new ideas and initiatives. The DNA team has begun to work with outside consultants to extend the growing cycle at Thanksgiving Farm, the collective name for The Center's cluster of local farms, and to produce more of the food consumed on campus. DNA is collaborating with The Center's occupational and speech therapists in projects like 3D Baking Company, in which residents create desserts for special events. They have worked with the pottery department to produce a small olive-oil tasting plate etched with the symbol for hope. Each season they launch more programs to bring students and their teachers into the fields to help with planting, picking and packaging vegetables, as well as feeding and handling livestock.

In these ways, The Center and DNA improve the quality of life for all concerned: residents, students and their families, staff and their families. The community is better. The care is better. The food is delicious. This is nourishment come full circle.

The Center grows a variety of legumes; director of farm operations Greg York; nutritionist Jennifer Franck, the assistant chief of DNA, and culinary director Peggy Parten; enjoying mealtime

The Conversation At The Center for Discovery, how to provide the best care is an ongoing exchange among staff nutritionists, therapists, chefs, farmers and caregivers.

> "Individuals with autism often have compromised immune systems. Seventy percent of the immune system is based in the gut. So **Food is Medicine**."

Center President and CEO Patrick Dollard, DNA chief Cesare Casella, DNA assistant chief Jennifer Franck, culinary director Peggy Parten, associate executive director Terry Hamlin, chief of clinical services Nicole Kinney, director of occupational therapy Coleen Visconti. There are—there are dozens of Center staffers who are key to improving the care of the residents. "The Conversation," a running feature found throughout the chapters of *Feeding the Heart*, brings together members of The Center community as they discuss their challenges and successes.

In this first Conversation, Dollard and Casella look back at The Center's history and forward to where it is headed.

Dollard first came to The Center for Discovery in 1980 when it was a small clinic with 25 staff members. Although the facility had expanded beyond its original mission to serve people with cerebral palsy, it still did not have a residential component or farming operation. Soon Dollard began to reimagine The Center as a home and safe place where the severely disabled could experience the outdoors, receive therapy and medical treatment and partake in simple activities.

Chef Casella stepped into the picture in the early 2000s when he was looking for a place to board a small herd of Italian cattle he had purchased to supply his New York City restaurant with the famous bistecca Fiorentina. Born in the Tuscan countryside, Casella had grown up in a culture with a deep ap-

Center President and CEO Patrick Dollard (left) and DNA chief Cesare Casella get "The Conversation" going.

Birth to 5 Symposium

Back in 1981, The Center was still known as the Human Developmental Services Center, United Cerebral Palsy Association of Sullivan County. That year The Center hosted one of the first symposia in the United States to raise awareness for parents and professionals about the care and treatment of developmentally disabled infants. Topics covered ranged from the reactions of families to the birth of a disabled child to the ethical issues of neonatology. The conference put The Center at the forefront of the effort to serve individuals with disabilities.

preciation of food and its sources. His parents owned and ran a trattoria, Vipore, and the family raised chickens and pigs, grew herbs, vegetables and olives. After Vipore won a Michelin star in 1992, Chef Casella moved to the United States for his next challenge. He was introduced to The Center at a moment when many of the farming, nutritional and culinary programs were already in place, but were still a work in progress.

Patrick Dollard: *In 1982 when I would visit the large institutions, food, it was a negative. Food was slop. In these settings the food, you couldn't get it out of your nostrils. I was a disruptor. I wanted to blow the system up and get to good food for my folks.*

Cesare Casella: *You were also very interested in food security.*

PD: *Yes, in the '80s and '90s, to me having a farm was a way to safeguard the food. I didn't want antibiotics or pesticides in the vegetables and meats. There wasn't the connection to elevating the food. When chefs became rock stars, it came together.*

CC: *When I showed up, the food at The Center was already respectable, and the staff was doing its best with quality, but no one was communicating. The nutritionists were like, "We need it to be healthy," but they weren't talking to the farmers and the cooks.*

PD: *Unfortunately, some present-day treatments look at autism as a psychiatric disorder. They use food as a reward for behavior. We have a huge segment of the autistic community*

that is obese. They are given M&M's and junk food. They come here and we give them good food and exercise and they lose weight and get healthier.

CC: *DNA really grew organically. Patrick, you and I got to know each other. I gave my Chianina cattle to the farm.*

PD: *Then it was a freight train; we took off. Cesare was able to dedicate time and I gave him authority. He focused in on season extension, the idea of expanding our growing season so we could consume our own produce for more of the year. He emphasized education for the staff, with the development of the DaVinci Master Chef program.*

CC: *The first time I came to The Center I was so impressed, but not in the expected way. Everything was so perfect. The people were so nice. I thought, "What is this? Caring for disabled like this?" I never saw that before. But I thought it was cool.*

PD: *It was something you wanted and The Center wanted you.*

CC: *When my wife and I slept at the meeting house the first time* and I woke up and I saw the Chianina on the hill, I was shaking. I thought, I am in Tuscany.

PD: *Cesare's relationship with The Center has gotten so much deeper in the past several years. It's a beautiful transformation for me, because I can see my staff seeing what he can bring. We are a disruptive program where we challenge convention.*

CC: *To me, The Center is a village.*

When I talk about Thanksgiving Farm, when Patrick works to revive the community of Hurleyville, it is to build something that doesn't exist. It is to build a place where our folks can live and blend in with the community. The people who live here grow in so many ways. It is incredible.

PD: *With Hurleyville, the goal is to see if we can bring back*

a community. You invest and make life better for everyone.

CC: *The animals, the fields, the people, they are all part of life here. At The Center, everything comes together. We grow the plants and breed the animals to eat, but we also need the animals for fertilizer, and they also eat the plants. It's all part of a circle. We are interconnected.*

Amy Hou

April Bloomfield

Johnny Iuzzini

Sue Torres

Pecko Zantilaveevan

Master chefs Nils Noren, Mark Ladner and
Kevin Garcia in the kitchen at The Michael Ritchie
Big Barn Event for a Sustainable Future

Heather Carlucci

Bill Telepan

The DaVinci Master Chefs

The DaVinci Master Chef program, created by DNA chief Cesare Casella, brings a piece of classical culinary training to The Center for Discovery.

In the four-star dining industry, novice chefs learn from masters as they rotate through the kitchens of famous restaurants in a series of working internships. The DaVinci Master Chef program adapts that formula by inviting the masters—some of New York City's most accomplished chefs—to The Center to hold seminars for DNA culinary staff. Throughout the year, Mark Ladner of Del Posto, Bill Telepan of Telepan, Carmen Quagliata of Union Square Cafe and a long list of other Master Chefs set up classroom in the Michael Ritchie Big Barn to share their experience and knowledge with DNA staff.

It is a program that not only has provided a learning opportunity to the staff, it has elevated the dining and nutritional experience of the residents and broadened The Center's community. "We believe in our chefs," says Chef Casella, "and we want them to stay with us. The more we give them opportunities like this, the more they will want to remain at The Center. If we believe Food is Medicine, we have to teach the best way to administer the medicine."

Named for Leonardo da Vinci, the artist, scientist and mathematician, the DaVinci Master Chef program covers everything from cooking skills to farming techniques. In each session the visiting chef demonstrates a number of dishes using seasonal ingredients harvested from Thanksgiving Farm. The recipes presented can be simple and spontaneous, inspired by

The DNA Culinary Staff

One of the longtime components of The Center's mission is to create a living environment that feels like home, which is why residents live family-style in small groups. And what makes a home feel more like home than the smell of dinner wafting through the halls? By preparing meals for the houses, DNA chefs become The Center's food ambassadors. They not only cook for and nurture the residents, they help coach them into better eating habits. Their enthusiasm can inspire picky eaters to embrace something new and make sure the nutrient-dense bounty of Thanksgiving Farm does its work. DNA residential chefs are also responsible for teaching the philosophy of Food is Medicine to non-culinary staff. When all employees understand the importance of healthy food, they transmit that energy to residents. In this team effort, the DNA residential chefs are on the front lines. The Center's goals could not be accomplished without them.

The DaVinci Master Chefs

Matt Abdoo, chef de cuisine, Del Posto restaurant

Robert Ambrosi, president, Ambrosi Cutlery, Ltd.

Dave Arnold, founder, Museum of Food and Drink; owner-partner, Booker and Dax Lab

Gaetano Arnone, sous chef, Babbo Ristorante & Enoteca

Franklin Becker, chef and partner, The Little Beet; author, *Good Fat Cooking*

April Bloomfield, chef and co-owner, The Spotted Pig, The Breslin, John Dory Oyster Bar, Salvation Taco, and Tosca Cafe

Heather Carlucci, Mother Industries New York

Paul Denamiel, executive chef and owner, Le Rivage

Laurent Dupal, Ceci Cela Patisserie

Michael Ferraro, executive chef and partner, Delicatessen

Simone Fracassi, Macelleria Fracassi

Kevin Garcia, executive chef, Giovanni Rana Pastificio & Cucina

Will Hickox, chef and owner, WPH Consulting

Johnny Iuzzini, owner, Sugar Fueled Inc.; author, *Dessert FourPlay* and *Sugar Rush*

Mark Ladner, executive chef, Del Posto restaurant

Kevin M. Lewis, Uncle and Hop Alley (Denver)

Maria Loi, chef and owner, Loi Estiatorio; author, *The Greek Diet*

Harold Moore, executive chef, Harold's Meat + Three

Nils Noren, chef and founder of Absolute Culinary

Francois Payard, FP Patisserie and Francois Payard Bakery

Carmen Quagliata, executive chef and partner, Union Square Cafe

Heather Bertinetti Rozzi, corporate pastry chef; author, *Bake It, Don't Fake It!*

Alain Sailhac, The International Culinary Center

Bill Telepan, chef and owner, Telepan restaurant; executive chef, Wellness in the Schools

Jacques Torres, Jacques Torres Chocolate

Sue Torres, EDJC Latin Flavors

Bill Yosses, Kitchen Garden Laboratory

Pecko Zantilaveevan, chef, The Four Seasons Restaurant

---

a walk through a vegetable field, or more elaborate, demonstrating techniques like braising or emulsifying. During and after the seminar, residential chefs are able to ask questions and taste the recipes, which are later adapted by executive chef Peggy Parten to be used in the menu cycle.

"We want to make sure the culinary team can execute the recipes, and also from a nutritional point of view that they reflect The Center's goals. But we try to keep them as close as possible to what the chef is doing," says Chef Casella.

The DaVinci Master Chefs have been as affected by the classes as the students. Most have returned multiple times to teach, and many have also volunteered to cook for the Michael Ritchie Big Barn Event for a Sustainable Future, DNA's annual fundraiser. "The tender love and care that goes into preparing one meal at The Center for Discovery goes way beyond cooking," says DaVinci Master Chef Sue Torres. "My visit with DNA has been the longest-lasting inspiration I have encountered in my life. It is still impacting me at this very moment."

Chef Casella plans to expand the DaVinci program to offer residential chefs more opportunities to learn outside their daily responsibilities. "This is one more way to extend our Seed to Belly philosophy," says Chef Casella. "With this kind of training for our staff, we are making sure that each seed we plant reaches its destination—the residents' bellies."

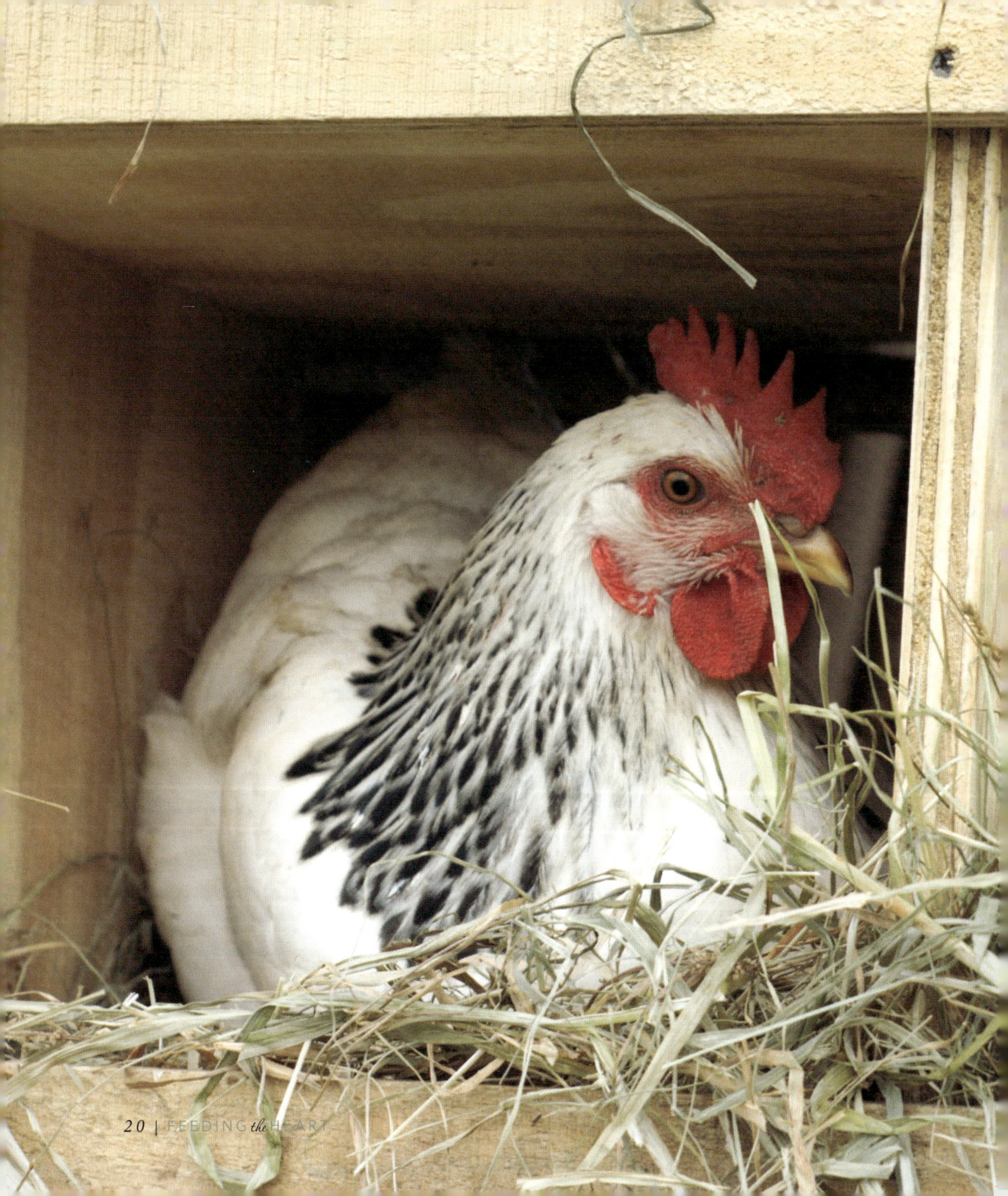

CHAPTER TWO:

The Chicken Coop

t's early morning, and up on Stonewall Preserve, against a backdrop of poplars, pines and oak, a small world is coming to life. In a sloping field ringed with wire, a flock of hens have begun their daily dance: scratching for food, preening, squabbling. Some are gregarious, others retreat to remote corners; some are bullied, others command respect. As one mother tends to her chicks, another hen-pecks the rooster, plucking feathers from his head and neck in an attempt to get her way. The birds vie for a place at the feed and water troughs dotting the field. To lay their eggs, hens seek refuge in a weathered coop built to look like an old railroad car and parked on a dusty patch of clay.

For the students at The Center for Discovery, this scene, bucolic, frenetic and affecting, is a living classroom. Each morning and afternoon the residents and their teachers make their way to the coops around the campus, to work and learn by interacting with the hens. They feed the birds and clean the nests. They reach into the nesting boxes and retrieve eggs still warm from the hen. After gently nestling the eggs in baskets, they participate in washing, sorting and packaging.

This is meaningful work, and therapy. The students establish deep bonds with the hens, and develop respect and patience. They hone their math skills by counting and weighing the eggs and learn the importance of being dependable, of showing up day in, day out and mastering tasks through repetition. While there is of course the occasional broken egg, the loss has been negligible—about one percent a year—while the gains are immense: In their interactions with the chickens, the children and adults blossom. When among the Light Brahmas, Rhode Island Reds, Barred Plymouth Rocks, or Black Australorps, their blood pressure normalizes and their hearts beat more slowly. They are calmer and more centered, thriving in the role of caregiver.

Recipes

The Coop

Cesare Casella: *It is so interesting to see the residents with the chickens. It's really happiness. They are so involved with the process. They take the eggs, they clean them, they sort them. In the home they see the cook make dishes with eggs.*

Patrick Dollard: *I know. The egg program is the whole package. It represents good food, good animal husbandry and it connects to the kids with autism. It is systems learning. We have a resident who came to us after some violent episodes, destroying property. People thought it was crazy to get him involved with the eggs, but it changed his life. It was a connection for him, caring for the animals.*

CC: *It's also something tangible. When you plant vegetables it's wonderful, but it takes so much time for the results. With the eggs, you see it happening in front of you. It's cause and effect.*

PD: *Like when you make a dish. You have the results immediately.*

CC: *Exactly, it makes you proud.*

Just as important, by working in the coops the residents are participating in their own nourishment. Stonewall Preserve, 100 acres of certified organic farmland, is one of a number of properties that make up The Center's Thanksgiving Farm. Each year, the coops on the farm produce 100,000 eggs which are used by the Department of Nourishment Arts, or DNA, to prepare meals for staff and residents.

Naturally high in protein, eggs are a nutrient-dense food. The farm's hundreds of fowl—chicks, pullets, laying and retired hens—forage for their own food, so the birds are healthy and strong. Their eggs in turn are higher in certain vitamins and minerals than most conventional eggs. The shells, some in beautiful hues of sky blue or minty green, are resistant and strong. Crack one open and the yolk will be deep orange-yellow and glossy, rich in vitamins A, D and K as well as omega-3s. Sample a dish made with the farm's eggs and you taste the hard work and dedication that goes into caring for the hens that laid them.

Chicken Chores

✔ Feeding and watering
✔ Cleaning nest boxes
✔ Calculating and recording egg logs
✔ Banding chickens
✔ Catching and moving chickens
✔ Putting up and mending fencing
✔ Printing egg labels
✔ Egg processing

Pontormo Salad With Wild Greens, Pancetta and Soft-Scrambled Eggs | *Cesare Casella* ~ Serves 4

A reclusive 16th-century painter who lived in Florence, Jacopo Pontormo has long been a favorite of Chef Cesare Casella, Chief of DNA. When Chef Casella was reading Pontormo's life story in the 1980s, he was inspired by the artist's musings on his garden view, the chicken coop and carne secca and came up with this recipe as a tribute. "It's not just the food we serve that makes a difference," says Chef Casella, who put the dish on the menu of his family's trattoria, Vipore, outside Lucca, Italy. "It's working with the soil, to be in a place that is healthy, to be out in the field. It's part of the therapy to feel better."

For the salad:

2 tablespoons extra-virgin olive oil

1 tablespoon mixed dried herbs
(use any combination of
rosemary, thyme, basil, savory,
chives, oregano or mint)

3½ ounces thinly sliced Italian
pancetta, cut into strips

6 eggs

Salt and fresh-ground black
pepper, to taste

4 cups washed mixed wild greens,
torn into bite-size pieces

For the Pontormo dressing:

1 tablespoon red wine vinegar

1 tablespoon balsamic vinegar

1 tablespoon red wine

¾ teaspoon salt

½ teaspoon freshly ground
black pepper

¼ cup extra-virgin olive oil

1. First prepare the dressing: In a small bowl, combine the vinegars and wine. Whisk in the salt and pepper, then the olive oil. Set aside.
2. Place the 2 tablespoons of olive oil, herbs and pancetta in a large frying pan over medium heat.
3. Beat the eggs with the salt and pepper.
4. When the pancetta is transparent, after 5 to 7 minutes, add the eggs to the pan, stirring slowly but continually. Cook to a very soft consistency. Do not hard-scramble.
5. Dress the greens with the Pontormo dressing, then mix with the eggs. Divide among four plates and serve immediately.

Sanitizing an Egg

After residents collect the eggs from the henhouses, they bring them to a special sorting room where they clean and package them for the kitchen and for sale at the Hurleyville Market, The Center-owned and -run shop in Hurleyville. Sanitizing is an especially important task. The residents first wash eggs in water and dry them with paper towels. Eggs are then placed in a solution of vinegar and water, where they remain for two minutes, after which they are removed and transferred to the refrigerator for eight minutes. Using a special diagram, residents then sort the eggs into jumbo, extra-large and large and place the eggs in cartons.

Lemon-Parmigiano Spaghetti Squash and Poached Eggs with Hollandaise | *Peggy Parten* ~ Serves 4

One of the challenges of organic farming in the Northeast is the short growing season. In Sullivan County, home to The Center, it's just six months, from May to October. To expand that window and provide produce for residents year-round, The Center in 2013 approached Eliot Coleman, a pioneer of organic farming and leading expert on four-season growing, and his daughter Clara. After an initial meeting with the Colemans, The Center's Department of Nourishment Arts, or DNA, organized a lunch showcasing The Center's work. This dish was the centerpiece of the meal.

For the spaghetti squash:

Yield: 4 cups

One 3- to 4-pound spaghetti squash
3 tablespoons extra-virgin olive oil
1 tablespoon freshly squeezed lemon juice
2 teaspoons freshly grated lemon zest
Pinch of sea salt
Pinch of freshly ground black pepper
½ cup grated Parmigiano-Reggiano cheese

1. Preheat oven to 400 degrees.
2. Halve the squash lengthwise, scoop out seeds and place the halves cut side down on a parchment-lined sheet pan.
3. Roast 45 minutes to 1 hour, until the squash is soft but still retains some texture. When the squash is done, turn the cut side up and allow to dry in the oven for 5 minutes, then remove.
4. Cool for 15 minutes before using a fork to scrape out the flesh, creating the spaghetti-like ribbons. Drain the squash in a sieve.
5. In a small bowl, mix the oil, lemon juice and zest, sea salt, black pepper and Parmigiano-Reggiano cheese and set aside.

For the hollandaise sauce:

Yield: 1 cup

While the squash is in the oven, make the hollandaise sauce. This easy recipe comes from an old *Houston Junior League Cookbook* belonging to Chef Parten.

4 large egg yolks
¼ teaspoon sea salt
¼ teaspoon sugar
¼ teaspoon Tabasco

¼ teaspoon dry mustard
2 tablespoons freshly squeezed lemon juice
½ pound (2 sticks) salted butter

1. Combine all ingredients except butter in a blender.
2. In a small pan, heat the butter until it begins to bubble.
3. Turn the blender to high speed and pour melted butter in a thin stream through the feed tube into the yolk mixture. It should thicken immediately. Set aside.

For the poached eggs:

2 to 3 teaspoons cider vinegar or white vinegar
1 tablespoon sea salt
8 large eggs

1. Pour 1 quart of water into a shallow 1.5-quart saucepan and bring to a boil, then lower the heat so it is no longer bubbling.
2. Add the vinegar and salt.
3. Working with the eggs one by one, crack an egg into a small cup. Bring the cup close to the surface of the hot water and gently tip the egg into the water. Be bold: If you hesitate and pour the egg in too slowly, you risk the white separating from the yolk.
4. Cook, taking care not to let the water boil, for 3 to 4 minutes, or until the white is opaque.
5. Remove the egg with a slotted spoon and, if desired, drain very briefly on a paper towel.

To assemble:

1. Place the squash in a microwave-proof bowl or sauté pan and warm through. Stir in the oil mixture until well combined.
2. Divide the squash among individual plates. With the back of a serving spoon, make two depressions in the spaghetti squash on each to hold the eggs in place.
3. Place a poached egg into each well and spoon hollandaise on top.
4. Serve immediately.

The Thanksgiving Farm and Community School

To involve older students more directly in the life of the farm, The Center has developed The Thanksgiving Farm and Community School. In this vocational program, students work with staff members to perform a variety of chores in the fields and barns. Those who show potential have their abilities and interests assessed by the education team in a two-week tryout; once accepted, they are given appropriate responsibilities, including mulching and pruning, post-harvest work in the wash barn, collecting compost daily from the kitchens on The Center's campus, and feeding the pigs. The program enriches students and residents on multiple levels, says Tom Mead, who oversees the school. "They learn to work with others, to follow through on tasks, endurance and to build a sense of pride."

Peppery Farm Eggs Baked with Parmigiano, Tomato and Basil | *DNA* ~ Serves 6

Working with the laying hens can be a deeply affecting experience for the residents and students. Chef Parten describes one resident who was nonverbal when he arrived at The Center. After a time working in the chicken coop, the young man said his first word, "egg." Here, a baked egg recipe that is fun to make and looks beautiful on the plate.

1½ tablespoons softened salted butter
3 fresh ripe tomatoes, cored and halved
12 large eggs
Salt
Freshly ground black pepper
6 tablespoons grated Parmigiano-Reggiano cheese
1 cup thinly sliced fresh basil leaves

1. Preheat oven to 400 degrees.
2. Generously butter the insides of six 8-ounce ramekins.
3. Place half a tomato, cut side up, into each ramekin. Season with salt and a generous grinding of black pepper.
4. Bake for about 15 minutes. Add two eggs to each ramekin, adjusting the tomato so that some of the egg white runs beneath it. Season with salt and pepper.
5. Return the ramekins to the oven and cook an additional 8 to 10 minutes. Remove from oven and top eggs with 1 tablespoon Parmigiano. Bake for another 4 to 5 minutes, or until the cheese has melted.
6. Remove from oven and garnish with basil. Serve.

Herb-Flecked Summer Squash and Zucchini Torte | *Kevin Garcia* ~ Serves 6

DaVinci Master Chef Kevin Garcia has taught many classes on Italian cuisine for The Center's culinary staff and also cooked at the Big Barn Event for a Sustainable Future, DNA's signature fundraising dinner held each fall. Here Garcia offers an Italian spin on quiche, spiked with herbs and splashed with a marinara sauce. Make this in the summer when zucchini is abundant.

1 pound thinly sliced zucchini
1 pound thinly sliced yellow squash
1 bunch thinly sliced scallions
1 dozen eggs, beaten
½ cup roughly chopped fresh Italian parsley
1 tablespoon roughly chopped fresh mint
½ cup roughly chopped fresh basil
3 tablespoons all-purpose unbleached flour
2 sprigs fresh thyme, leaves only
4 tablespoons grated Parmigiano-Reggiano cheese
1 teaspoon sea salt
½ teaspoon freshly ground black pepper
¼ cup olive oil

1. Preheat the oven to 350 degrees.
2. Place all the ingredients except the olive oil in a mixing bowl and stir until thoroughly blended.
3. Warm the olive oil in a 10- to 12-inch ovenproof skillet. Pour in the egg-vegetable mixture.
4. Let the eggs cook until the bottom has set. Using a heat-resistant spatula, push away the sides and tilt the pan to let the liquid egg flow underneath. Repeat, working your way around the pan until there is no liquid left.
5. Place skillet in the oven for 10 minutes to finish cooking. Cut into wedges and serve with marinara sauce.

For the marinara sauce:

Makes 1 quart

1 tablespoon extra-virgin olive oil
1 teaspoon minced fresh garlic
Pinch crushed red pepper flakes
2¼ cups whole peeled canned tomatoes (preferably San Marzano)
2¼ cups tomato puree
1½ teaspoons dried oregano
1 teaspoon herbes de Provence
1 tablespoon chopped fresh basil or 1 teaspoon dried
1 teaspoon freshly ground black pepper
1 teaspoon sea salt

1. Warm the olive oil in a 1½-quart pot and add the garlic and crushed red pepper. Cook over a medium-low flame until the garlic turns white. Do not allow to brown.
2. Add the tomatoes and cook briefly.
3. Add the tomato puree, dried herbs, black pepper and salt. Simmer for 30 minutes, stirring to prevent sticking.

The Conversation Establishing Trust

Associate executive director Terry **Hamlin, Ed.D., P.D.,** who has worked at The Center since 1983, oversees program operations, management, curriculum design and program evaluation. She is also the author of *Autism and the Stress Effect*, a step-by-step guide to help families reduce the stress and anxiety levels in their children's lives. Here, Dr. Hamlin and Cesare Casella discuss The Center's philosophy on the role of diet and exercise in people with autism.

Cesare Casella: *Many of the residents who come here have a self-limiting diet. The foods are high carbohydrate or high sugar. It is so widespread.*

Terry Hamlin: *Definitely. That's what they crave. Unfortunately, education takes advantage of that. In order to get kids to sit, teachers give them cookies. So they get half an Oreo if they sit for ten minutes.*

Many arc young kids—five, six, seven years old—and have aggressive behaviors so that school districts are saying, "We can't manage them." Families are saying, "We don't know what to do." The kids have sleep disorders, gastrointestinal problems, they aren't able to function normally.

CC: *When they come here and we do the blood profiles, they are out of whack because their diets are so poor. It affects their behavior. That's why we want them to eat a whole-foods, plant-based diet.*

TH: *The transition isn't always* easy, but we start slowly and gain their trust. It can be a few months or a few years. We had one boy who came here and only ate Goldfish crackers and rice. It took two years to get him eating our menu. We let the child smell the food, play with it. We create a structured routine. Once they are accepting of us, it makes a huge difference.*

CC: *It is more than simply what is on the plate.*

TH: *It is a holistic approach, nutritional, environmental, therapeutic, social. Most of the kids have never had a friendship. We structure the program to develop friendships. Even if it is one friend, it makes all the difference in the world. We teach how to interact in a small group and in a large group.*

Cesare, you have helped so much with our staff. They don't always understand how important food is, how to prepare it to maintain its nutritional value. You've educated

Associate executive director Terry Hamlin and DNA chief Cesare Casella in The Carrus Cafe at The Center for Discovery.

the staff on how to feed themselves and the residents.

CC: *One of the advantages we have here at The Center is that we have complete control of the food we serve. We have our own farm, which gives us great flexibility.*

TH: *It is almost like a laboratory.*

CC: *I know. Last year, we grew a lot of broccoli and cauliflower, then froze it to serve when it wasn't in season. That was great, but this year we aren't going to freeze. We have worked to* extend the season with hoop houses, so this year, we will be able to serve fresh broccoli and cauliflower for longer. Every day we are improving the process.

TH: *The nutritional component goes hand in hand with energy regulation. How much do kids move during the day? We know they tend to be sedentary and that's not healthy. Exercise is critical. So is diet and reduction of stress factors.*

CC: *It's a very common sense approach, for everybody.*

The HealthE⁶

Building blocks of the program at The Center for Discovery

....

Environment: Creating positive physical, natural and temporal surroundings

Eating, Food and Nutrition: Emphasizing a whole-foods, plant-based diet

....

Energy Regulation: Making sure everyone exercises and sleeps

....

Emotional Self- Regulation: Giving residents the tools they need to deal with daily life

....

Evidence-Based: Conducting research and teaming with academics and hospitals to be at the forefront of developments

....

Education: Teaching those inside and outside our community about the critical factors in the health of people with autism

Wake-Up Taco with
Thanksgiving Farm Cilantro-Jalapeño Salsa | *DNA*

This dish, with its soft eggs and cheese rolled into a warm tortilla, is Mexican comfort food at its best. It also happens to be protein-dense, making it an ideal breakfast in the residences. Prepare it in late summer when tomatoes are at their peak. "Use the extra salsa with chips later," recommends Chef Parten.

For the salsa:

Yield: 2¼ cups

1 pound fresh tomatoes

2½ tablespoons finely
    diced red onion

2 tablespoons chopped
    fresh cilantro

1 fresh jalapeño pepper

⅓ teaspoon minced garlic

½ teaspoon sea salt

1 tablespoon fresh-
    squeezed lime juice

1. Core and dice tomatoes into ¼-inch pieces.
2. Slice jalapeño in half, remove core and seeds (for spicier salsa, incorporate the seeds) and mince.
3. Place the tomatoes, onion, cilantro, jalapeño, garlic, salt and lime juice in a glass bowl and toss.

For the tacos:

Yield: 6 tacos

4 tablespoons salted butter

6 corn tortillas

6 eggs

⅓ cup whole milk

Salt

Freshly ground black pepper

¾ cup grated sharp cheddar cheese

Thanksgiving Farm cilantro-
jalapeño salsa

1. Heat one tablespoon butter in an 8-inch skillet over medium heat until melted. Swirl to coat the pan.
2. Adding one tortilla at a time, cook briefly until softened, then flip and heat for about 20 seconds more.
3. Set tortillas aside on a warm plate and cover with a clean towel. Continue until all tortillas are hot.
4. Crack eggs into a glass mixing bowl and beat until they turn a pale yellow. Add the milk and season with salt and pepper.
5. Heat a heavy-bottomed nonstick sauté pan over medium-low heat. Add two tablespoons butter and let it melt.
6. Whisk the eggs vigorously and pour into the hot pan.
7. Let the eggs cook until the bottom has set. Using a heat-resistant spatula, push away the sides and tilt the pan to let the liquid egg flow underneath, working your way around the pan. Repeat until there is no liquid left.
8. Stir eggs and remove from heat.
9. To assemble, place ⅓ cup scrambled egg onto a warm tortilla. Top with 2 tablespoons of grated cheese and 2 tablespoons of salsa. Fold tortilla in half. Serve.

The Conversation The Right Setting

Chief of clinical services Nicole Kinney, director of occupational therapy Coleen Visconti and occupational therapist Jessica Piatak discuss the role of assistive technology.

Nicole Kinney: *When a child or adult comes in we do an intensive evaluation.*

Coleen Visconti: *We are looking at their diet and ability to control movement. Are they able to sit at a table? Does their wheelchair provide support?*

NK: *Depending on the strength of their grip, we provide different utensils. If they are on pureed foods, there are a variety of bowls sizes for spoons. If we don't have the right fit, we can develop one.*

CV: *We might make a raised platform so it is easier to get food into the mouth or put the platform on a tilt. If they can't reach the floor, we add foot support so they have a stable base.*

Jessica Piatak: *We are addressing underlying medical and motor issues. They might have problems chewing or acid reflux.*

NK: *It is part of the process of building trust.*

The French Fry Method

For some residents who live at The Center, mealtime has been stressful, and there may be little or no intrinsic pleasure in food. They are picky or disinterested eaters who need to be coached just to get through a meal. If they've come from a large institution, they may balk at food with a pronounced flavor or texture. For DNA, it is important to prepare meals that are more than just "healthy"—the dishes need to entice the residents and, most important, feel familiar.

The process is gradual, and DNA works hard to help residents transition to eating and enjoying meats, grains and vegetables grown on The Center's organic farm or by one of DNA's local suppliers. A good transition food is french fries, which most residents have tried, often at a fast-food restaurant, before they came to live at The Center.

DNA's strategy is to use familiar tastes to convert an eater to healthier habits. In the case of french fries, the kitchen would start with organic potatoes, frying and freezing them, then frying them again, the way fast-food restaurants do. In the houses, the fries might be served in a bag to mimic the fast-food experience. The next step would be thicker-cut fries prepared the same way. Over time the chef would move to fries that are baked, and after that switch to sweet potatoes. Now DNA is working on a fermented ketchup to serve with those fries that contains some gut-healthy probiotics.

CHAPTER THREE:

The Field & Garden

The sound of joy is coming from the wash barn.

It is a crisp November morning in a work shed on Thanksgiving Farm and strains of Journey's "Don't Stop Believing" are pulsating from a boom box on a shelf. A class of six young women and their teachers are sorting hundreds of pounds of just-picked vegetables, inspired by the upbeat melody and the fall bounty around them.

There are crates upon crates of sunny-orange carrots. Armfuls of frilly kale and velvety spinach spill out from their sacks. Dozens of stalks of Brussels sprouts, picked clean, are lined up across the bed of an old truck. The space is cavernous, with soaring ceilings, yet intimate and familiar. On a far wall, a shadowy row of slickers, rubber boots beneath them, await rainy-day field work. A blackboard is filled with details of the day's business. Students, teachers and farmhands alike are bundled up against the cold and the wash barn has the feel of an old-fashioned harvest party, but there is so much more going on here.

"When you see the residents with their behaviors, you'd think not much is going to happen," says the director of farm operations, Greg York, referring to productivity. "But in the morning I can leave a to-do list on the blackboard and I know they'll get it done."

If anything defines The Center for Discovery's holistic approach to caring for the residents who come to live and work here, it is Thanksgiving Farm, a rich patchwork of farms that surround the residences and research facilities. There are vegetable, fruit, herb and corn fields and animal pastures, in all about 250 acres. This is a commercial-scale operation that feeds students and staff alike and supplies a CSA with crops Sullivan County is known for, from beets and broccoli to radishes and zucchini. The fields also serve as classrooms in which teacher and student collaborate and social centers where residents and their families gather. For the residents the fields create a bridge between nutrition and therapy, between sustainability and education, between the great outdoors and healthy, delicious food.

At the Department of Nourishment Arts, or DNA, this holistic approach is referred to as Seed to Belly, as residents and staff are involved in every step of the production cycle, from the sowing of fields to the harvest to the preparation and eating of local, seasonal ingredients. The residents know the gratification of pulling a carrot from the soil, laying down a bed of garlic, of shearing corn kernels from their cobs. They plant the seeds that grow, produce and feed their bellies. They discuss what they've harvested with the residential chefs who prepare their meals. "You can't get more meaningful than supplying your own food," says Peggy Parten, The Center's executive chef. "That's what farming is. It gets people outside. There is routine and regularity to it. That's good for everyone."

While the farm has always been an integral component of The Center's work, in recent years the agency has expanded significantly the number of hands-on programs that take students into the fields and barns. Now, in addition to participating in long-standing activities like working with laying hens, students are involved in planting, caring for and harvesting crops.

There is a seeding room with specially designed tables that allow students of many different abilities to plant seeds. There is a farm apprentice program. Recently a group of students began tending a patch of carrots, learning to work together, to focus, to organize and count. Similarly, during twice-weekly classes in the wash barn, students develop balance and flexibility, fine motor skills, teamwork and concentration. They bend to pick up tools, move crates, flex their hands, learn to pull on gloves, bundle and count. When the program started, the classes were just an hour and students were able to work just ten minutes at a time. "Now the class is three hours long and the students can go a half hour to forty minutes without a break. That's huge," says their teacher, Petra Stephens.

This is not just make-work. During the wash barn session, students assist in cleaning, sorting and bundling tasks that would otherwise fall to the farmers. They are also participating in The Center's commitment to biodynamic agriculture, in which soil fertility, plant growth and livestock care are connected, just as the residents are to the land itself.

Jean-David Derreumaux, The Center's biodynamic expert, sums up the holistic experience: "It's feeding the soil, it's the landscape. It's a notion of place. As human beings we are connected to this place. In these fields, there are life forces."

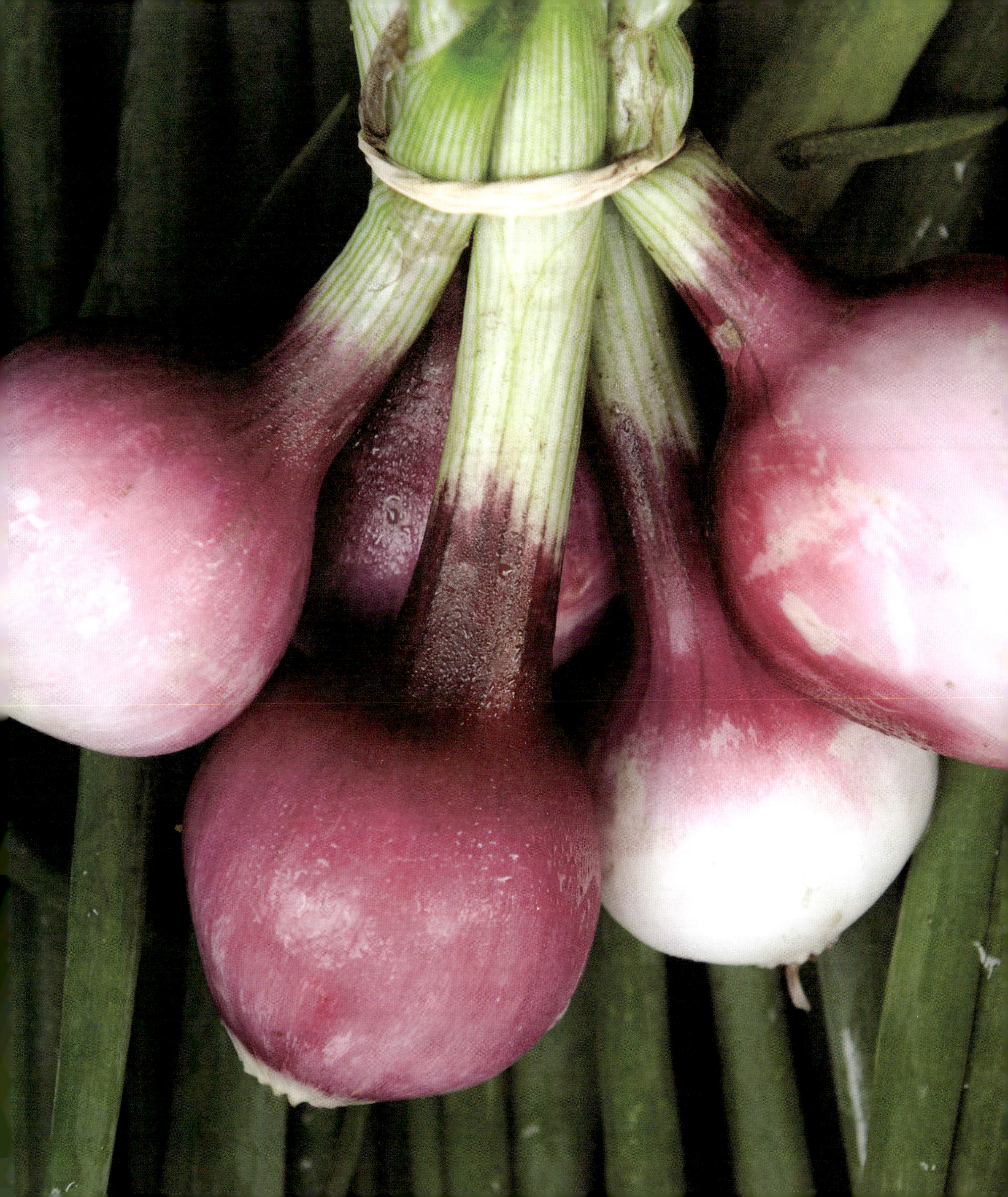

Soups

Autumn Harvest Red Pepper Stew | *DNA* ~ Yield: 2½ quarts

In the fall, drive around Thanksgiving Farm and you will see glossy red bell peppers growing in the field. This sweet, simple soup is a great source of vitamin C.

2⅔ tablespoons
    salted butter
2⅔ tablespoons extra-
    virgin olive oil
8 red bell peppers
    cored, seeded and
    halved lengthwise
1⅓ cups diced onion
1⅓ cups thoroughly
    washed and chopped
    leek, dark green tops
    reserved for another use
⅓ teaspoon sea salt
⅔ teaspoon freshly
    ground black pepper
4 small potatoes,
    peeled and sliced
6⅔ cups chicken stock
2⅔ tablespoons chopped
    fresh chives

1. Place the butter and olive oil in a soup pot and warm over medium-low heat until the butter has melted. Add the bell pepper, onion, leek, salt and pepper. Cover and cook until the vegetables begin to soften, about 10 to 15 minutes.
2. Add the potatoes and stock. Bring to a simmer, uncovered, and cook until vegetables are tender, about 30 minutes.
3. Transfer the soup, in batches, to a blender and process until smooth. (This will result in a silkier texture than using a food processor.)
4. Return the soup to the pot and heat through.
5. If too thick, add a little more chicken stock or water.
6. Garnish with chopped chives and serve.

Baked Potato Soup With Havarti
and Thanksgiving Farm Bacon | *DNA* ~ Yield: 2½ quarts

2 pounds potatoes
4 tablespoons butter
4 tablespoons extra-
    virgin olive oil
5 cups chopped
    yellow onion
4 cloves garlic, minced
2 teaspoons sea salt
1 teaspoon fresh-ground
    black pepper
4 cups homemade
    chicken stock
4 cups water
8 slices thick-cut bacon
1 cup milk
1 cup sour cream
2 cups grated Havarti
    cheese
4 tablespoons thinly
    sliced scallions

Everything you put on your baked potato is in this soup, says Chef Parten. It is a big favorite in the houses in fall and winter. Because the soup is rich, a cup-size serving is perfect.

1. Preheat the oven to 375 degrees.
2. Scrub the potatoes and pierce in several places with a fork. Set them directly on the oven rack and bake until very tender when pierced with a fork, about 1 hour. Let cool completely and set aside.
3. In a soup pot, place the butter, oil, onion, garlic and salt and sauté over medium-low heat until vegetables are softened, about 10 minutes.
4. Add the stock and water. Bring to a simmer over medium heat and cook until onion and garlic are very tender, about 15 minutes.
5. While the soup simmers, arrange bacon on a sheet pan and put in oven. Bake for 15 minutes or until crisp. Transfer to a plate lined with paper towels to drain and cool. Crumble when cool and set aside.
6. Divide the potatoes into two equal portions. With one, cut the potatoes in half lengthwise and use a large spoon to scoop out the flesh in a single piece from each half. Then cut the flesh into ½-inch cubes. Add the skins to the remaining whole potatoes.
7. Coarsely chop the whole potatoes and added skins and place in the soup pot.
8. Working in batches, puree the contents of the pot in a blender until very smooth.
9. Return the puree to a clean soup pot and reheat over a medium-low setting. Whisk together the milk and sour cream until smooth, then whisk that into the puree, along with half the cheese. Stir in the diced potato and season with salt and pepper.
10. The soup should be fairly thick. If necessary, thin with a little water. For serving, garnish each bowl with the remaining cheese, bacon and scallions.

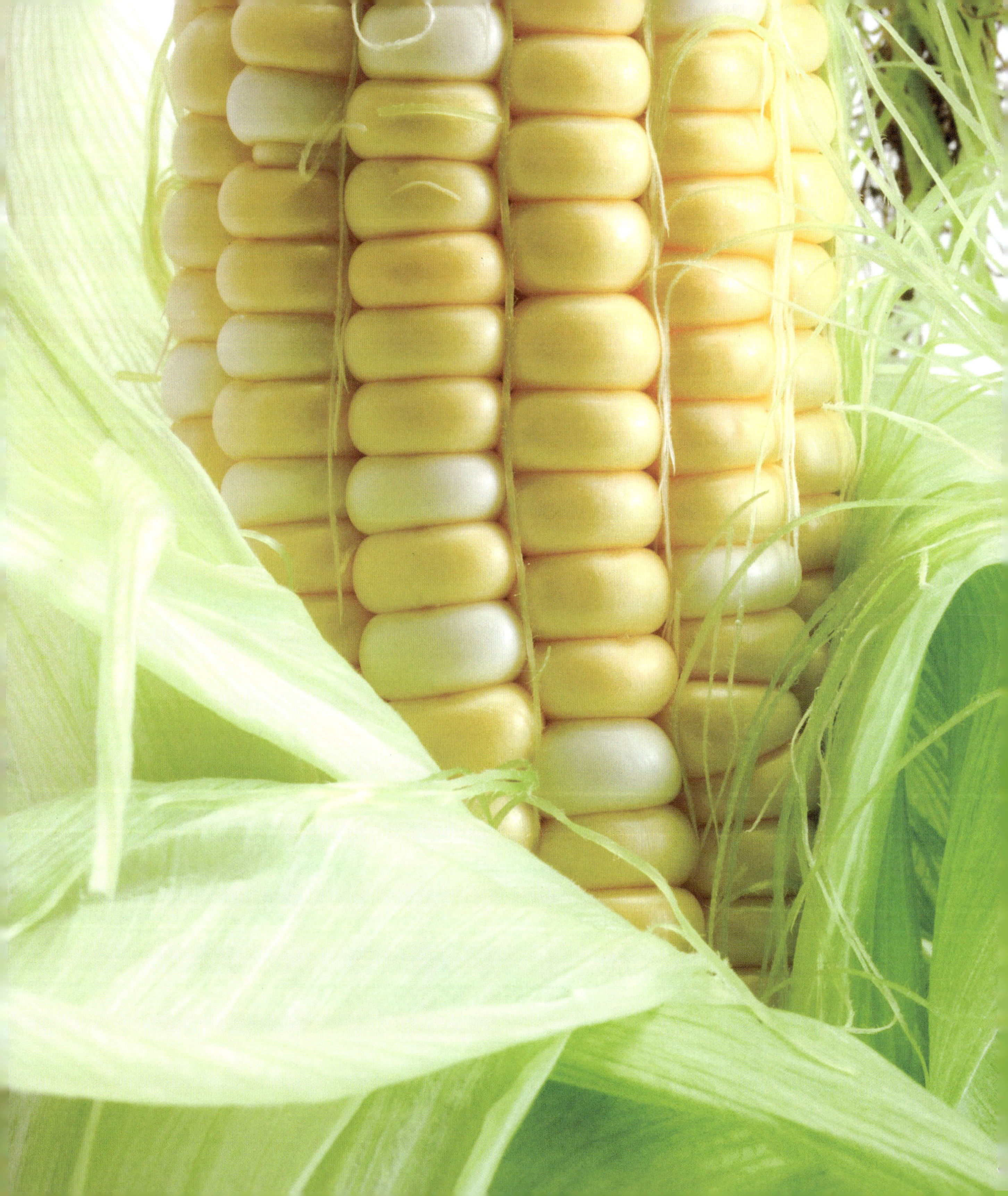

Corn Chowder with Summer Herb Salad | *DNA* ~ Yield: 4 cups

Many residents love their chefs so much they will eat whatever they make, says Chef Parten. There is not much arm-twisting with this sweet summer chowder, adapted from *Fine Cooking* magazine. Toss the salad together at the last minute so the ingredients maintain their vibrant colors.

For the chowder:

2 ears corn, husked, silk removed

4 tablespoons sweet butter

⅔ cup diced onion

4 teaspoons minced garlic

2 teaspoons sea salt

1 teaspoon granulated sugar

⅔ teaspoon freshly ground
 black pepper

2 sprigs fresh Italian parsley

2 sprigs fresh thyme

½ bay leaf

4 cups water

For the salad:

1 cup chopped fresh basil

1 cup chopped fresh dill

⅔ cup chopped
 fresh chives

6 tablespoons chopped
 fresh tarragon

2 tablespoons extra-
 virgin olive oil

½ teaspoon sea salt

Pinch of fresh-ground
 black pepper

2 fresh tomatoes, cored
 and chopped

1. Stand ears of corn upright in a large bowl. With a small paring knife, shear kernels into bowl, starting from the top.
2. Remove ⅓ cup of the kernels; place in a bowl and set aside.
3. Using a butter knife, press down the length of the cobs to squeeze out the milky liquid into the bowl with the kernels.
4. Discard 1 cob. Snap the other in half and put aside to flavor soup.
5. Melt butter in a soup pot over medium-low heat. Add onion, garlic, salt, sugar and pepper. Cook, covered, until onion is translucent, about 5 to 7 minutes.
6. Add the bowl of corn kernels with their milky liquid to the soup pot. Cook, covered, until corn is tender, about 10 to 12 minutes.
7. Tie the parsley, thyme and bay leaf with kitchen twine (or tie into a bundle of cheesecloth) and add to soup along with reserved cob half and water.
8. Bring the mixture to a boil. Reduce heat and simmer, uncovered, until slightly thickened, about 30 minutes.
9. Remove and discard herb bundle and cob.
10. Puree the chowder in small batches in a food processor until creamy.
11. Return the puree to the pot, add reserved corn kernels and simmer over medium heat, uncovered, until the kernels are just tender, about 5 minutes.

1. In a large bowl, combine all ingredients, adding the tomatoes last, and toss. Place a generous mound in the center of each bowl of chowder and serve.

The Thanksgiving Farm CSA

Stop by The Carrus Institute on a Tuesday afternoon and you will see a bustling greenmarket under the eaves, with staff and residents of Sullivan County picking up boxes of fresh produce from the Thanksgiving Farm Community Supported Agriculture (CSA) initiative. In late spring, the boxes will brim with greens, peas and radishes. In summer there will be an abundance of tomatoes, eggplants, peppers, cucumbers and zucchini. Fall will bring out the roots—potatoes, carrots, parsnips—and squashes.

The program, like other CSAs around the country, is subscription-based and provides members with a weekly share of the Thanksgiving Farm bounty. Typically it's about 15 pounds a week of ultrafresh naturally grown produce that is free of synthetic herbicides and pesticides. For employees, who qualify for a reduced-

Jim Cashen, the director of outdoor education, at the CSA.

fee membership, there are multiple benefits.

"The farm, the CSA, is a way to connect all the people at The Center—the residents, the families, the employees," says Jim Cashen, the director of outdoor education, who points out there is also a pick-up on Main Street in Hurleyville on Saturdays. "The CSA is part of our social life."

Creamy Carrot-Ginger Soup | *Franklin Becker* ~ Serves 4

DaVinci Master Chef Franklin Becker focuses on healthy eating at his gluten-free The Little Beet restaurants in New York City. He is also the author of a number of cookbooks, including *Good Fat Cooking*. Chef Becker demonstrated this soup at a master class in part because he was inspired by the land at Thanksgiving Farm. "Ginger and carrots both grow in the ground and are full-flavored," he says. "One spicy one sweet, so they have a natural affinity to one another. The soup is simple, delicious and very nutritious."

¼ pound salted butter
1 pound peeled and
    sliced carrots
2 cloves garlic, chopped
½ teaspoon ground
    turmeric
¼ teaspoon ground cumin
1 tablespoon grated
    peeled fresh gingerroot
Sea salt
Freshly ground
    black pepper
Water to cover
Sautéed chunks of
    lobster, shrimp or
    scallops, optional
Chopped chives

1. Place the butter, carrots, garlic, turmeric, cumin and ginger in a large pot and sauté until the vegetables are soft.
2. Cover with water and simmer until the carrots are tender.
3. Working in batches, place the carrots in a Vitamix and puree until smooth (you can use a food processor, but the soup will be chunky). Return the soup to the pot and heat through.
4. Adjust seasoning. For a thinner soup, add a little water. Stir and serve.
5. For added body, garnish with sautéed chunks of lobster, shrimp or scallops. Finish with a sprinkling of chopped chives.

Cucumber-Dill Soup

Bill Telepan ~ Serves 6

....

DaVinci Master Chef Bill Telepan, a pioneer in locavore cooking, is the owner of a namesake New York City restaurant. He created this soup for his wife, who loves the contrast of the puree and crunchy chopped cucumber, but it also seemed like a natural for a DaVinci Master Class because it provided a flavorful way to showcase Thanksgiving Farm's great cucumber harvest. "I know it's a really nutritious soup, so it's a great dish to feed the residents," says Chef Telepan.

6 cucumbers, peeled and seeded
1 bunch scallions
1 bunch fresh dill, stems removed
1 clove garlic
Juice of 3 lemons
3 cups plain yogurt
1 cup Greek yogurt
1 teaspoon sea salt
½ teaspoon freshly ground black pepper
Dash Tabasco sauce

1. Thinly slice half the cucumbers and half the scallions and set aside.
2. Coarsely chop the remaining cucumbers and scallions and transfer to a large bowl. Mix in the dill, garlic, lemon juice, and yogurts. Season with salt and pepper.
3. Puree mixture in a food processor.
4. Combine the puree with the reserved cucumber and scallion, adjusting seasoning with salt and pepper.
5. Chill for at least 2 hours before serving.

Cauliflower-Coconut Soup
With Shrimp | *Nils Noren* ~ Serves 4

DaVinci Master Chef Nils Noren has cooked for guests at the Big Barn Event for a Sustainable Future for many years and calls it one of his favorite celebrations of the year. "I am honored to be part of it and get to meet all the people that make The Center for Discovery so special," he says. Chef Noren made a version of this cauliflower soup for the event one year and described it as "extra-special due to the great produce from the farm." The soup, he says, "is rich yet light, has spice and character, and garnishes can easily be changed seasonally."

2-inch piece of fresh ginger,
   peeled and sliced
2 stalks lemongrass, thinly sliced
3 kaffir lime leaves
2 cups strong chicken stock
3 16-ounce cans unsweetened
   coconut milk

1 head cauliflower,
   cut into florets
Lime juice, to taste
6 large shrimp, cleaned
Cilantro leaves
2 tablespoons thinly sliced
   scallion

DaVinci Master Chef Nils Noren *says this soup "is rich yet light, and has spice and character, and garnishes can easily be changed seasonally."*

1. Place the ginger, lemongrass, kaffir lime leaves and chicken stock in a large pot and bring to a boil. Turn off the heat and let sit for an hour, then strain. Discard the solids.

2. Return the stock to the pot and add in the coconut milk and pieces of cauliflower. Bring the liquid to a simmer and cook until the cauliflower is completely soft. It is better to cook it a bit longer than to undercook it. If too much liquid evaporates, just add a little water. Stir from time to time to make sure the bottom doesn't burn.

3. Place the liquid with the cauliflower in a food processor and pulse until smooth. Season with salt. (For a silkier texture you can pass the puree through a fine sieve.)

4. Bring a medium pot with salted water to a boil, turn off the heat, and add the shrimp. Check the shrimp after 5 to 6 minutes to see if they're cooked through. Remove at once to avoid overcooking, as this toughens them.

5. To serve, gently heat the soup, then remove from the burner and season with lime juice (the lime juice will lose its fresh taste if overheated).

6. Ladle into bowls, divide shrimp among them, garnish with cilantro and scallion.

It is all part of having the organism function as a whole. Fertility is key.

Biodynamic Farming

"Farming has been part of the human experience forever. It is part of what connects human beings to plants and animals. It is a concept that goes beyond nutrition. It is nutrition of the soil, the landscape. It is a notion of place."

—Jean-David Derreumaux

Jean-David Derreumaux (above) oversees the healing gardens and the biodynamic farm program at The Center for Discovery.

Everything is connected. Humans to the earth. The earth to animals. Animals to people. People to people. Food to health. Health to well-being. Well-being to the environment and the world at large. That is the philosophy of the Department of Nourishment Arts, or DNA.

Nowhere are those concepts more evident than in the fields of Thanksgiving Farm, where the farmers, residents and Center staff cultivate produce and livestock according to the principles of biodynamics, and in turn care for and feed themselves and the community.

Biodynamic farming is a spiritual approach to food production that intertwines agriculture, ethics, nutrition and sustainability. It was developed in the 1920s by Austrian educator and social activist Dr. Rudolf Steiner, who wanted to bring a holistic consciousness to farming. A farm was not just a farm. It was connected to the community. It was dependent on the earth. The first

CSA was created by biodynamic farmers. At The Center, biodynamic principles of planting, fertilizing and caring for livestock and crops shape not only the work of the farmers, but also that of the residents, other staff and the community around Hurleyville. The principles produce foods that are above all safe and free of pesticides and other pollutants, but that are also gorgeous, nutrient-dense and delicious. Crack open the egg of a chicken raised on Thanksgiving farm and its yolk will be an intense orange, like the sun. The kale is a deep purple-green, so sweet it could be candy. The bacon is velvety and subtle, a reflection of

In biodynamic farming, special preparations are made from medicinal plants and animal manure. Here, the Center staff bury preparations in advance of winter.

"Where I see the biggest impact is how families see their children," says Patrick Dollard, president of The Center for Discovery

happy, humanely raised pigs.

The ability of Thanksgiving Farm to produce these foods is all the more remarkable considering the fact that the soil of Sullivan County is not naturally rich. Many farmers have struggled with the rocky fields and short growing season. But Center president Patrick Dollard was committed to the idea that Food is Medicine, and that growing and serving foods that could heal was part of The Center's mission of caring for residents in a holistic way. He first converted the farmland to organic production, and then over the years began incorporating biodynamics, a system that translates into caring for the world at large.

"Where I see the biggest impact is how families see their children," says Dollard. "They are transformed by nature. The best thing I can say is when I first started bringing people here, 60 percent refused because they thought their kids were too vulnerable. They couldn't handle getting rain on their faces. To be in the fields. But that has totally changed. We've evolved and the kids and their families have evolved with us."

Today, visitors can see the farmers and staff embracing the rituals of biodynamic farming, which turn on marrying plants and animals in a balanced cycle. The plants provide food for the animals, and the animals, through

their manure, enrich the soil. Under the direction of Jean-David Derreumaux, The Center's expert on biodynamics, the staff and residents participate in making special compost preparations that are used throughout Thanksgiving Farm.

I n fall, the staff comes together to stuff cow horns with manure, then bury them to form a compost that is later mixed with water and is used as a fertilizer. They also make biodynamic fertilizing preparations from yarrow and chamomile flowers, nettles, oak bark. These get-togethers are festive and fun, like an old-fashioned barn raising where neighbors pitch in to help each other. Derreu-

maux likens the fertilizer that results from the preparations to homeopathic medicine for the plants. "It is to get the plants to be all they can be. The carrots have more sugar. The other vegetables have more vitamins. It enhances the maturing process," he says.

It is all part of having the organism function as a whole, adds Derreumaux. Fertility is key.

On the farm you have soil, plants and animals. Plants tend to take away from the soil. Animals take plants but give back manure. "You need both. You work with animals and plants to build and mine the fertility. Compost is a key ingredient. This is the notion of organism that Patrick has for us."

Derreumaux examines a biodynamic preparation—a ball of dandelion flowers which has been buried in the garden for the winter.

Sides

Summer Squash, Cacio e Pepe Style | *Will Hickox* ~ Serves 4

6 tablespoons extra-virgin olive oil

1 tablespoon thinly sliced garlic

½ teaspoon sea salt

¼ teaspoon freshly ground black pepper

¼ teaspoon crushed red pepper flakes

6 cups julienned yellow squash (can be sliced lengthwise to look like spaghetti)

¼ cup finely grated Parmigiano-Reggiano cheese

½ cup finely grated Pecorino Romano cheese

This summer squash dish was inspired by the classic Italian pasta *cacio e pepe*, which is sauced simply with grated cheese and ground black pepper. DaVinci Master Chef Will Hickox says he wanted to make something gluten-free for The Center's residents. "It's very simple and it pleases all palates, from children to adults," says Chef Hickox. "Because of the cheese in the sauce it is very easy to achieve the same consistency as the classic dish. Another bonus: it's very fun to cook, and you can get better every time you cook it."

1. Start with a cold pan. Add half the olive oil, the sliced garlic and the salt. Warm the oil until garlic starts to bubble but does not color.
2. Add black pepper and chili flakes, then squash. When the squash starts to soften, add a small amount of water. Be careful not to overcook the squash or it will become mushy.
3. Slowly stir in the cheeses, starting with the Parmigiano. Stir constantly until there is a creamy emulsified sauce. If the squash begins to dry out, add a splash of water.
4. To finish, add the remaining olive oil, season with additional salt and pepper, and top with a small amount of cheese. The dish should be peppery and creamy, but not oily.

Roasted Carrots with Cumin and Lime | *DNA* ~ Yield: 2 cups

In 2014, The Center introduced three of its classes to carrot farming, and once the plants were mature, the students were in the field twice a day to harvest. As of late fall they had pulled up 10,000 carrots. When carrots are delivered to the residences, some house chefs use the opportunity to discuss the vegetables and the students' role in cultivating them. A half cup is the standard serving size for this dish, but you might want to make extra, as your guests will be asking for more, according to Chef Parten.

1. Place a baking sheet in the oven and preheat to 425 degrees.
2. Peel the carrots, then cut in half and quarter each half lengthwise. Cut the sticks into ½-inch pieces. Place carrot pieces in a large mixing bowl and squeeze lime juice over them. Drizzle with half the olive oil (2½ tablespoons) and sprinkle with cumin, garlic and salt and pepper to taste. Toss well to coat evenly.
3. Remove the baking sheet from the oven. Pour on the remaining olive oil and tip it one way and another to coat.
4. Arrange the carrots on the baking sheet in a single layer and roast for 10 to 15 minutes. Using a spatula, turn the carrots and roast another 10 minutes, or until tender when pierced with a fork. Plate and serve with wedges of lime.

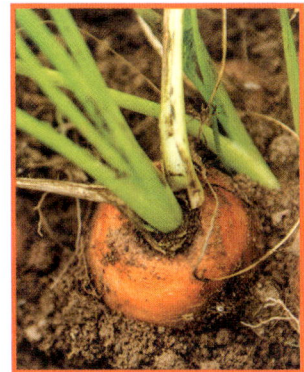

8 large carrots (enough to make 4½ cups sliced carrots)
Juice of 1 lime
5 tablespoons extra-virgin olive oil
2 teaspoons ground cumin
4 teaspoons minced garlic
2 teaspoons sea salt
1½ teaspoons freshly ground black pepper
Lime wedges, to garnish

The Carrot Program

One of the most recent initiatives by DNA to integrate farm work into daily life revolves around planting carrots. In season, residents and students spend an hour and a half at a time in different fields, where they first plant, then later harvest the crop. It is hard work that involves loosening soil with a pitchfork, pulling hard until the orange shaft springs from the ground and collecting the carrots in baskets.

"The residents love harvesting carrots," says Greg York, director of farm operations. "They could do it all day." Though some of the students who participate in the program have challenging behaviors, they are focused and productive in the carrot patch. "They are able to do this without distraction. It's amazing," says York.

Ginger-Spiked Pickled Cucumber | *Will Hickox* ~ Serves 4

2 tablespoons
   whole coriander
   seed, toasted
2 tablespoons whole
   black peppercorns,
   toasted
2 tablespoons whole
   fennel seed, toasted
2 sprigs fresh thyme
½ teaspoon crushed
   red pepper flakes
2-inch piece of fresh
   gingerroot, peeled
   and sliced into
   thick rounds
2 cups white vinegar
1 tablespoon sea salt
2 tablespoons
   granulated sugar
1 cup peeled and
   sliced cucumber

The Center is committed to prolonging the season's harvest using a variety of preservations methods, including pickling. Chef Hickox's brine-based recipe for cucumbers aligns with that initiative. "Through Cesare and the rest of the staff at The Center I have learned not only how to cook more-nourishing food, but also why those foods are so great for our bodies. It has been an absolute pleasure participating in the DaVinci Master Chef program," says Chef Hickox.

1. Tie spices, thyme sprigs and ginger in a piece of cheesecloth.
2. Place the vinegar, spice bag, salt and sugar in a small nonreactive pot and bring to a boil. Let cool.
3. Pour the cooled brine over the cucumbers and let sit for a minimum of 1 hour, but preferably overnight, before serving. This is a lightly pickled cucumber. Do not leave in brine longer than 2 days.

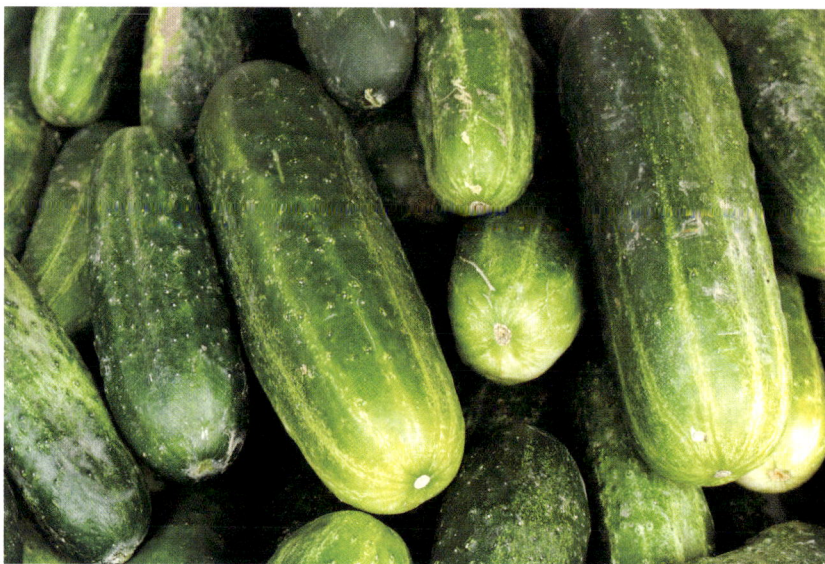

Italian Summer Vegetables
"In Scapece" | *Carmen Quagliata* ~ Serves 4

Master Chef Carmen Quagliata is the executive chef and partner at Union Square Cafe in New York City. He is known for his simple Italian-inspired cuisine, like this sautéed-vegetable platter. He suggests turning the dish into a light summer dinner by serving it with a fresh loaf of Italian bread and canned sardines.

1 large perfectly ripe tomato, peeled and chopped coarsely, saving all the juice

1 large clove garlic, chopped fine

15 to 20 fresh basil leaves, torn

1 red bell pepper, roasted, peeled and chopped fine

¼ cup red wine vinegar

Salt

Freshly ground black pepper

1 medium zucchini

1 Japanese eggplant

Flour for frying

¾ cup grated pecorino cheese

1 quart extra-virgin olive oil

1. To make the vinaigrette, mix the tomato, garlic, basil, bell pepper and vinegar with salt and pepper. Set aside.
2. Cut the zucchini and eggplant into ¼-inch slices. Place in a mixing bowl and toss with salt and pepper. Let stand 10 minutes.
3. Place a small mound of flour in a separate bowl. Add the vegetables and toss so they are lightly coated. Arrange them on a parchment-lined sheet tray
4. Heat the olive oil in a large high-sided skillet until it begins to shimmer. Add slices of zucchini and fry until golden brown, then place on a sheet tray (no towels—we want the olive oil). Repeat the process with the eggplant.
5. Sprinkle the vegetables with a little more salt. Then shower liberally and evenly with the grated pecorino.
6. Spoon a little of the vinaigrette onto a platter and spread out with the back of the spoon. Layer ½ of the vegetables shingle-style across the platter, then spoon on more vinaigrette. Layer more vegetables and then spoon on the rest of the vinaigrette .
7. Drizzle with olive oil and let sit at room temperature for at least an hour before serving.

Aloo Gobi
with Pistachio Chutney | *Heather Carlucci* ~ Serves 4

In an effort to serve the residents who are on a gluten-free diet, DNA asked DaVinci Master Chef Heather Carlucci to create a dish without grain, and she came up with this version of aloo gobi, a traditional dish in Indian cuisine. "This is a hearty dish that goes well with a number of proteins and, of course, it is easy to grow all of the ingredients locally," says Chef Carlucci, who sees the seminars as a learning experience not just for the students, but the instructor too. "I get to learn as much as I teach."

For the aloo gobi:

1 tablespoon canola oil
1 teaspoon whole cumin
1 medium onion, sliced
2 cloves of garlic, finely chopped
1 Thai chili, finely chopped
2 teaspoons grated fresh ginger
1 medium potato, cut into 1-inch pieces
⅓ teaspoon ground turmeric
1 teaspoon ground coriander
1 teaspoon garam masala
2 teaspoons paprika
1 tablespoon salt
1 head cauliflower, cut into 1-inch florets
Water, as needed
1 tablespoon finely chopped fresh cilantro

1. Place the oil in a wide shallow pan or rondeau. Add the cumin and cook over medium heat until it sizzles.
2. Add the onion, chili, garlic and ginger. Sauté until brown.
3. Add the potato, turmeric, coriander, garam masala, paprika and salt. Cook for 10 minutes.
4. Add the cauliflower and a splash of water. Cover.
5. Cook until potato cubes are tender and cauliflower is cooked through, about 5 to 10 minutes.
6. Sprinkle with cilantro and serve.

For the pistachio chutney:

"This pistachio chutney is great on everything," says Chef Carlucci. Unlike many condiments, the chutney doesn't contain sugar.

2 teaspoons ground coriander
1 teaspoon ground cumin
1 tablespoon olive oil
16 ounces plain yogurt
2 Thai chilis, halved lengthwise (remove seeds for a milder chutney)
2 cups fresh cilantro leaves
1 tablespoon lime juice
1½ cups unsalted shelled pistachios
2 teaspoons salt

1. Place the coriander, cumin and oil in a frying pan and heat until the mixture sizzles. Let cool.
2. In a blender, mix the fried spices, yogurt, chilis, cilantro, lime juice, pistachios and salt. Pulse until smooth.
3. Serve with the aloo gobi or any dish that could use a savory-spicy kick.

The Conversation Empathy

Patrick Dollard: *It's always good to discuss empathy in the same context as sympathy. Sympathy is feeling sorry for someone. Empathy is a deeper understanding and the ability to feel what someone else is going through. We are attempting to drive home the notion that people can get better and are valued.*

Cesare Casella: *One of the first meetings I had with you, you were talking to the board and saying how people need to give to The Center not because they feel sorry for the residents but because they believe in creating a better life for them. If you give to Yale or Harvard or another school, it's because you feel education*

is important. It is the same with The Center. It is because you believe in the food, in the beautiful surroundings, in the farm and the gardens. It is believing in the philosophy of making people's lives better.

PD: *Food is such a good example. It is universal. It is something that drives a sense of meaning. The opposite was true when I started working. Food was an afterthought. It was slop they threw in front of people. DNA is going deep in the care system. Care and value is put in front of everyone three times a day.*

CC: *The staff works hard to create a better life for the residents and students. Success is when you see they are happy.*

PD: *The folks we are caring for are not always valued in society. People ask me all the time, Why are you growing organic food for those people? Why biodynamic? I say, Why not? I continue to have that conversation with a lot of people, "Why are we so fancy and fussy?" Part of this work is to create new life passages where maybe we can make people feel there are greater possibilities out there if we really work hard at it.*

Salads

Lentil Salad With Balsamic Vinaigrette and Marinated Cucumber | *Will Hickox* ~ Serves 6 to 8

Chef Hickox says this salad contains great prebiotics and that it turns beans, "which most people consider heavy," into a light and healthy salad. To break up the work, you can prepare the marinated cucumber a day ahead.

For the marinated cucumber:

2 cups rice wine vinegar

1 cup water

3 tablespoons salt

½ cup fresh gingerroot, peeled and cut into ¼-inch slices

Crushed red pepper flakes, to taste

Mirin or granulated sugar, to taste

½ cup shallots, shaved thin

4 cups cucumber, sliced in ¼-inch-thick rounds

1. Place the vinegar, water, salt, ginger and red pepper flakes in a saucepan and bring to a boil. Taste and season with more salt if necessary, or more vinegar or water.
2. Add mirin or sugar for a little sweetness.
3. Place the shallots in a generous-sized bowl and pour in the boiling liquid to cover.
4. Cool completely and add in the cucumber. Be sure to keep the vegetables completely submerged, using a plate to hold down if necessary.
5. Let marinate for one hour or up to two days before using.

For the balsamic vinaigrette:

2 cups balsamic vinegar

½ cup whole-grain mustard

⅓ cup extra-virgin olive oil

Salt and freshly ground pepper

1. Pour the vinegar into a nonreactive heavy-bottomed saucepan and adjust the burner to medium-high. Watch carefully as it reduces and lower the temperature if necessary. Be careful not to scorch or the vinegar will become bitter.
2. Reduce to ½ cup. (If you are using syrupy aged balsamic, you will use

less to start with and reduce less.) Cool.

3. Place the reduction in a small bowl and whisk in mustard.
4. Whisk in the olive oil in a slow, steady stream. The sauce should not break.
5. Season the dressing with salt and pepper. If necessary, add more balsamic for acidity or water if the dressing is too thick. Set aside.

For the lentil salad:

½ cup diced white onion

¼ cup diced carrot

¼ cup diced celery

½ cup extra-virgin olive oil

Salt

Freshly ground black pepper

4 cups dried lentils

2 cups mixed herbs (parsley, cilantro, mint, chives), stems removed, roughly chopped

4 cups mesclun lettuce medley

1. Place the onion, carrot and celery in a mini food processor and pulse to a chunky paste.
2. Transfer the paste to a large soup pot and add the olive oil. Season with salt and pepper and sweat slowly over medium heat until the vegetables are tender, sweet and transparent, but not browned.
3. Stir in lentils, mixing thoroughly. Add enough cold water to cover.
4. Slowly bring water to a simmer and cook until lentils are soft but not broken. Depending on the variety of lentils used, this could take 20 minutes or more.
5. Add water sparingly as needed throughout cooking.
6. When lentils are cooked, let cool. Drain in a colander if there is excess liquid.
7. Place lentils in a bowl and toss with cucumber-shallot mixture, herbs and lettuces. Season with salt, pepper and dressing. Serve at once.

The Healing Garden

In Colonial times, the land around Hurleyville, where part of The Center for Discovery is now located, was known for its healing plants. Goldenrod, used to make a tonic to thin the blood, was so plentiful it came to support an export business and was shipped as far away as China. Burdock, considered a treatment for everything from dry skin to fevers, grew wild. So did chamomile.

Today DNA has cultivated three healing gardens that connect The Center's work today to the area's rich medicinal history. The gardens grow over 60 different herbs, flowers and ornamental shrubs that are used by the kitchen staff. Some are transformed by biodynamic expert Jean-David Derreumaux into teas, salves and balms to treat residents. In class, students also go into the healing gardens to fork garlic beds, lay mulch or just enjoy the peaceful setting. They also package the herbs and teas, which are sold in The Center-owned Hurleyville Market in Hurleyville.

Kale Caesar | *Kevin Lewis* ~ Serves 6

For Kevin Lewis, holding a DaVinci Master Chef seminar was a learning as well as a teaching experience. He knew how to create recipes that were tasty, but also wanted to come up with dishes that were sensitive to the dietary needs of the residents and could be easily integrated into The Center's menu cycle.

After consulting with nutritionist and assistant DNA chief Jennifer Franck about the role of the digestive tract in health, Chef Lewis turned his thoughts to recipes that incorporate raw garlic. The first that came to mind? A simple, flavorful anchovy-garlic vinaigrette he made with DNA Chief Cesare Casella. The perfect foil for the dressing, he thought, would be "a kale salad that would deliver great nutrition and all kinds of minerals. It would be a crowd pleaser, a recipe that the cooks at DNA could not only make for the guests but also for themselves."

For the anchovy vinaigrette:
3 tablespoons red wine vinegar
5 tablespoons extra-virgin olive oil
3 cloves garlic, mashed into a paste
5 salt-packed anchovy fillets, rinsed

1. Place all ingredients in a food processor and blend until smooth. Set aside.

For the salad:
2 heads Tuscan kale, cleaned, stemmed and chopped fine
Zest of 1 lemon, slivered

1. Place kale and half the lemon zest in a bowl
   and mix well with anchovy dressing.
2. Spoon the salad onto serving plates and garnish with more zest. Serve.

Golden Beet Salad with Avocado, Mint Chiffonade and White Balsamic Vinaigrette | *Franklin Becker* ~ Serves 4

"I love beets and wanted to give a clean, fresh approach to them," says DaVinci Master Chef Franklin Becker.

1. First, make the dressing: In a small bowl, whisk together the orange juice, vinegar, olive oil, salt and pepper. Set aside.
2. Remove tops from the beets and reserve for another use.
3. Prepare the two types of beets in separate pots to preserve colors. Place the golden beets together with 1 bay leaf, 1 sprig thyme, 1 clove garlic and 1 tablespoon sea salt in the first pot and add enough water to cover. Repeat with the red beets.
4. Bring both pots to a boil and reduce to a simmer. Cook until beets are fork-tender. (This can take up to 45 minutes.) Turn off the flame and allow beets to cool in the water.
5. To avoid staining your hands, wear gloves. Peel the beets and cut into uniform cubes.
6. Place the beets in separate glass bowls and toss each with some of the dressing. Marinate overnight.
7. Combine the yogurt with the coriander and cumin, zest of lemon and season with salt and pepper. Set aside.
8. Remove the beets from the refrigerator. Combine in a large bowl and add the cut avocado.
9. Smear a little of the yogurt mixture on each serving plate and top with the beet-avocado mixture. Serve chilled or at room temperature.

For the vinaigrette:
Juice of 1 orange
1 tablespoon white balsamic vinegar
3 tablespoons extra-virgin olive oil
Sea salt
Freshly ground black pepper

For the salad:
½ pound golden beets
½ pound red beets
2 bay leaves
2 sprigs fresh thyme
2 cloves garlic
2 tablespoons sea salt
1 Hass avocado, diced
1 teaspoon Italian parsley chiffonade
1 teaspoon mint chiffonade
Sea salt
Freshly ground black pepper

For the yogurt sauce:
6 tablespoons low-fat Greek yogurt
¼ teaspoon ground coriander
¼ teaspoon ground cumin
Zest of ¼ lemon

Radish Panzanella | *DNA* ~ Yield: 6 cups

To make this Italian-inspired bread salad, Chef Parten uses watermelon radish, a non-starchy winter vegetable that grows well on Thanksgiving Farm and is easily stored. Diners get excited by its bright pink color, which makes it an easier sell at dinnertime, she says. "You can cut it very thin and put it in ice water and it curls like a potato chip. The chip is something everyone is familiar with. It can win them over. Every bit helps." The homemade croutons seal the deal.

For the radish mixture:

8 watermelon radishes
3 tablespoons extra-virgin olive oil
¾ teaspoon salt
1 pound sourdough bread, crust removed and cut into 1-inch cubes

For the dressing:

¾ cup extra-virgin olive oil
⅓ teaspoon fresh-ground black pepper
12 rinsed and finely chopped anchovy fillets
6 cloves garlic, finely chopped
Pinch crushed red pepper flakes
2 tablespoons chopped fresh Italian parsley
3 ounces shaved Parmigiano-Reggiano cheese

1. Preheat oven to 400 degrees.
2. Remove tops and roots from radishes and quarter lengthwise.
3. Toss with 3 tablespoons of olive oil and salt. Place on a sheet pan and roast for 10 minutes. Remove from oven, then combine radishes and bread cubes in a large bowl.
4. Place the remaining ¾ cup olive oil, anchovies, garlic and red pepper flakes in a small skillet over medium heat for 4 minutes.
5. Pour the anchovy-garlic mixture over the bread and radishes. Toss. Spread on a sheet pan and return to oven until croutons are lightly toasted and radishes are tender, about 7 to 10 minutes.
6. Allow mixture to cool, then toss with parsley and Parmigiano-Reggiano. Serve.

Green Bean Salad with Citrus Vinaigrette | *DNA* ~ Yield: 4 cups

Green beans are one of the vegetables residents prepare in the wash barn, packaging them for distribution throughout The Center. "The wash barn has been a huge success for us," says farmer Greg York. "It's amazing."

1 pound green beans, trimmed and cut into 1-inch pieces
1½ teaspoons finely grated orange peel (zest orange before squeezing it)
¼ cup freshly squeezed orange juice
1½ tablespoons balsamic vinegar
½ teaspoon granulated sugar
½ teaspoon Dijon mustard
½ teaspoon sea salt
¼ cup extra-virgin olive oil
¼ cup diced red onion
⅛ teaspoon freshly ground black pepper

1. In a large saucepan, bring salted water to a boil and cook beans until just crisp-tender, about 3 minutes.
2. Drain and set aside. In a jar with a tight-fitting lid, shake together remaining ingredients.
3. Toss beans with dressing shortly before serving.

The Seeding Room

What does it take for Thanksgiving Farm to transplant 18 acres' worth of vegetables, 65 types in all?

The Center for Discovery residents.

In the Seeding Room of the Thanksgiving Greenhouse, residents make up the unseen manpower behind the farm's cultivation of dozens of crops.

As part of a vocational training program, residents work at specially designed tables to fill pocketed flats with dark earth, level the soil, then transfer seeds to each pocket. Depending on the volume of seeds, there might be just two students on duty, or as many as four or five. They are focused, often encouraged by classical music played by the staffer who oversees the Seeding Room. Some days they fill 30 to 40 flats over a five-hour period. "They develop great skills and the farm benefits just as much as the guys do," says director of farm operations Greg York.

Pasta & Grains

Pasta Cooked in Pommarola Sauce | *Cesare Casella* ~ Serves 8

"In the summertime, I love going out in the field at Thanksgiving Farm where the tomatoes are because they are beautiful," says Chef Casella. "I just pick one and eat it right there." This dish concentrates the flavor of the tomato by cooking the pasta right in the sauce.

6 tablespoons extra-virgin olive oil

6 cloves garlic, peeled and crushed

1 stalk celery, chopped

1 carrot, peeled and chopped

1 cup chopped red onion

½ teaspoon crushed red pepper flakes

1 cup fresh basil leaves, sliced into ribbons

3½ pounds fresh plum tomatoes, cored and chopped

1 pound whole wheat penne or other short pasta

1. In a large saucepan, heat the olive oil, garlic, celery, carrot, onion, pepper flakes and half the basil over medium heat. Cook until carrots are soft, about 25 minutes.
2. Add the tomatoes and cook for 40 to 50 minutes. Add the remaining basil. Remove from heat.
3. Puree the mixture in a food processor. Return the sauce to the pan and cook for another 30 minutes. Season with salt and pepper. If sauce is too thick, add a little water.
4. With sauce still simmering, add the pasta. Cook, stirring frequently, until pasta is just barely tender, 15 to 20 minutes.

Root Cellar Pasta e Fagioli | *DNA* ~ Yield: 5 cups

When The Center started moving toward organic food a decade ago, some employees were unenthusiastic, according to Chef Parten. "For them, organic meant bean sprouts and tofu," she says. Now that staff members have seen what a difference eating local and organic can make, there is more buy-in. Plus, DNA tries to come up with instant-appeal dishes like this Root Cellar Pasta e Fagioli that are familiar and home-style, "things that are spectacular in their eyes and our eyes," according to Chef Parten.

2½ tablespoons extra-virgin olive oil
1 small onion, chopped
1 small potato, peeled and chopped
⅓ cup grated peeled celeriac
¾ pound butternut squash, peeled, seeded and chopped
Pinch crushed red pepper flakes
⅓ teaspoon dried rosemary
2½ cups homemade vegetable stock
⅓ teaspoon sea salt
½ teaspoon freshly ground black pepper

1 ounce Parmigiano-Reggiano cheese rind, if available
3 ounces gluten-free (such as quinoa) elbow pasta
2 tablespoons chopped Italian parsley leaves
2 cups home-cooked cannellini beans and their cooking liquid
⅓ cup grated Parmigiano-Reggiano cheese

1. Place olive oil and onion in a soup pot and sauté over medium heat until translucent. Add potato, celeriac and squash. Stir to coat.
2. Add crushed red pepper, cooking briefly. Then add rosemary, vegetable stock, salt, pepper, and, if you have it, Parmigiano-Reggiano rind.
3. Bring the mixture to a boil, then lower to a simmer and cook until all vegetables are very soft.
4. While soup is cooking, add pasta to boiling salted water and cook until just barely tender. Drain, rinse and set aside.
5. Remove cheese rind from the soup and discard. Add the beans and their cooking liquid. Remove from heat and allow to cool slightly.
6. Transfer half the soup to a food processor and pulse until smooth. Add the puree back into the soup pot and reheat to a simmer.
7. Just before serving, add the pasta and stir to distribute evenly. Garnish each serving with fresh parsley and 1 tablespoon grated Parmigiano-Reggiano.

Penne with Swiss Chard Ragù | *Mark Ladner* ~ Serves 6

For the ragù:

6 tablespoons extra-
    virgin olive oil
1 medium onion, peeled
    and cut in ¼-inch slices
4 cloves garlic, smashed
    and peeled
1½ pounds Swiss chard,
    washed, trimmed and
    cut into ¼-inch ribbons
1½ teaspoons kosher salt
½ cup water
6 tablespoons cold salted
    butter, cut into pieces
¾ teaspoon freshly
    ground black pepper

For the pasta:

4½ tablespoons kosher salt
1½ pounds whole wheat
    penne pasta
¾ cup of the pasta
    cooking water
1⅛ cup grated Parmigiano-
    Reggiano cheese
¾ cup fresh bread crumbs
    toasted in olive oil

DaVinci Master Chef Mark Ladner decided to make a dish with Swiss chard because he knew it was plentiful at the farm and because it is one of the most vitamin-rich vegetables out there. Swiss chard also falls into the category sometimes referred to as "low FODMAP"—Fermentable, Oligosaccharides, Disaccharides, Monosaccharides And Polyols—meaning it is lower in certain carbohydrates that are poorly absorbed by the small intestine.

"I like working as a DaVinci Master Chef because it gives me the opportunity to connect with people I would not otherwise have the pleasure of working with," says Ladner, who is the chef at the four-star Del Posto restaurant in New York. "It has also been a wonderful learning experience, and in teaching I have come to learn much more about nutrition from my friend Cesare Casella and The Center's highly professional staff."

1. Combine the oil, onion, garlic, and chard in a large pot. Cook over medium-high heat, stirring occasionally, until the onion and chard begin to soften, about 5 minutes. Season with kosher salt.

2. Add the ½ cup water, cover, reduce heat to low and cook, stirring occasionally, until chard is very tender, about 20 minutes.

3. Add the butter, stirring until it melts, then season with pepper and remove from the heat. (Ragù can be made up to two days ahead; reheat before adding pasta.)

4. In a large pot, bring 8 quarts salted water to a boil. Add pasta and cook until just al dente.

5. Drain pasta, reserving a cup of the cooking water.

6. Add the pasta and some of the cooking water to the chard ragù. Stir and toss over medium heat until pasta is well coated, adding more pasta water if needed to loosen the sauce.

7. Stir in the cheese. Transfer the pasta to a serving bowl and scatter the bread crumbs over the top. Serve with additional grated cheese on the side.

Farro Risotto | *Michael Ferraro* ~ Serves 4 to 5

DaVinci Master Chef Michael Ferraro, the chef at Delicatessen in New York, was impressed by DNA's food program and the deep involvement residents have in cultivating ingredients. In making this risotto, he wanted "to create a dish that utilized the pristine products that come off the farm" while considering "the nutritional needs of some of the residents, therefore trying to incorporate many farm vegetables."

1. Preheat oven to 350 degrees.
2. Place the squash, 1 tablespoon of the olive oil, the oregano, 1 clove minced garlic, 2 sprigs of the thyme, and 1 tablespoon shallot in a medium bowl. Season with sea salt and ground pepper and toss together.
3. Spread the mixture on a sheet tray in a single layer. Place on oven rack and roast until tender and lightly caramelized, about 20 minutes. Set aside.
4. While squash is roasting, place 1 tablespoon olive oil, 1 tablespoon minced shallot and 1 clove minced garlic in a large sauté pan over medium heat until the shallot begins to soften. Add Swiss chard chiffonade. Season with salt and pepper. Reserve.
5. In a large rondeau pot, add the remaining tablespoon olive oil, 1 tablespoon butter, 2 tablespoons diced shallot, and 2 thyme sprigs. Cook over medium heat until shallot is translucent, about 3 to 4 minutes.
6. Add farro and stir so each grain is coated. Add white wine. Cook for 3 minutes, stirring, until 80 percent of the white wine has been absorbed.
7. While stirring, add hot stock to the farro, ladle by ladle, over the course of 20 minutes. Reserve 2 cups of stock.
8. Check farro for doneness. The grain should be slightly al dente. At this point you will add the squash, chard, Parmigiano and mascarpone cheeses, remaining butter and chiffonade of basil.
9. Add remaining stock as needed. Consistency of farro should be loose and creamy. Season with sea salt and fresh-ground pepper.
10. To serve, ladle farro into bowls. Drizzle each with extra-virgin olive oil and garnish with scallion chiffonade.

2⅓ cups peeled, seeded and diced summer squash

3 tablespoons extra-virgin olive oil, plus more for finishing

1 sprig oregano, leaves removed and chopped

3 small cloves garlic, minced

4 sprigs thyme

4 tablespoons minced shallot

Sea salt

Freshly ground black pepper

¾ cup Swiss chard chiffonade (leaf only)

2½ tablespoons butter

12 ounces farro

⅔ cup white wine

2 quarts chicken or vegetable stock, at a simmer

1½ cups mascarpone cheese

⅔ cup grated Parmigiano-Reggiano cheese

⅓ cup basil chiffonade

⅛ cup scallion chiffonade (green only)

Mains

Summer Vegetable Chili with Brown Rice Pilaf | *Harold Moore* ~ Serves 6

The aspiration of Harold Moore, executive chef of Harold's Meat + Three in New York City, is to "cook what people want to eat." For his DaVinci Master Chef class, Chef Moore prepared this robust but simple chili that reflects The Center's philosophy of food that is seasonal, local and plant-based. If you like your chili on the mild side, you can leave out the jalapeño.

For the chili:

1½ tablespoons extra-virgin olive oil

1 cup diced onion

½ cup diced carrot

½ cup diced celery

1 cup diced green bell pepper

Sea salt

Freshly ground black pepper

½ cup diced leek, white and
    light-green parts only,
    thoroughly rinsed

½ cup green beans, cut
    into 1-inch pieces

½ cup diced peeled and
    seeded yellow squash

½ cup diced zucchini

½ cup corn kernels

½ cup diced tomato

1 jalapeño pepper

2 tablespoons chili powder

2 tablespoons ground cumin

2 tablespoons onion powder

2 tablespoons garlic powder

14.5 ounces canned fire-
    roasted tomatoes

2 tablespoons cornstarch

Sour cream, for garnish

Shredded cheddar or Monterey
    Jack cheese, for garnish

1. In large pot over medium heat, combine the onion, carrot, celery and bell pepper. Season with salt and pepper.
2. Allow the vegetables to sweat, stirring occasionally, for 5 to 7 minutes.
3. When the mixture becomes slightly translucent, add the remaining vegetables, one type at a time. Allow each addition to become tender before adding the next. It will be about 25 to 30 more minutes.
4. Place the whole jalapeño over an open flame and char the outside. When all the sides are blackened, remove from the flame and set aside.
5. When all the vegetables are tender, stir in the chili powder, cumin, onion powder and garlic powder. Cook for 3 to 4 minutes, or until the spices become fragrant.
6. Break up the canned tomatoes with your hands and add 1 cup water.

Add the charred jalapeño.

7. Bring the liquid to a simmer and cook, stirring and tasting occasionally, for about 15 minutes. When the liquid has attained the desired amount of spiciness, remove the jalapeño from the pot and discard.
8. Adjust the burner to high and bring the liquid to a boil.
9. In a small bowl, combine the cornstarch with 2 tablespoons cold water and stir until it is dissolved. Add to the chili and stir.
10. When the mixture thickens, remove from the heat.

For the brown rice pilaf:

2½ tablespoons unsalted butter
1½ tablespoons finely chopped shallot
1½ cups brown rice
Sea salt
Freshly ground black pepper
3¾ cups water or vegetable stock
3 small garlic cloves, smashed
2 or 3 fresh thyme sprigs
2 bay leaves

1. Melt 1 tablespoon butter in a large saucepan over medium heat.
2. Add the shallot and cook until translucent, stirring occasionally.
3. Add the rice and stir until the kernels are glossy and slightly toasted. Season with salt and pepper.
4. Add the water or stock, garlic, thyme, and bay leaves. Bring to a boil.
5. Reduce to simmer, cover with a tight-fitting lid and cook for 40 minutes.
6. Remove the pot from the heat and allow the rice to sit, covered, for 10 minutes.
7. Remove the lid and discard the garlic, thyme, and bay leaves. Fluff the rice with a fork.
8. Stir in the remaining butter. Taste and adjust for seasoning. Spoon into individual serving bowls and ladle chili on top.
9. Garnish each serving with sour cream and shredded cheese.

Soft Lentil Tacos
With Chipotle and Cumin | *DNA* ~ Serves 6

1 cup du Puy French lentils

½ teaspoon sea salt

2 tablespoons extra-
virgin olive oil

1 cup diced onion

1 tablespoon minced garlic

1 teaspoon chili powder

1 teaspoon ground cumin

1 teaspoon ground
coriander

Pinch dried oregano

2½ cups homemade
vegetable stock or water

1 teaspoon canned
chipotle pepper

⅓ cup sour cream

1 teaspoon of the
adobo sauce from
the canned chipotle

3 cups thinly shredded
romaine lettuce

¾ cup Thanksgiving Farm
Cilantro-Jalapeño
Salsa (see page 30)

1½ cups grated
cheddar cheese

12 corn tortillas

Like all beans, lentils benefit from being soaked for at least four to six hours before they are cooked. The process helps break down complex carbohydrates and makes the lentils easier to digest, which is important for residents. They should be soaked in salted water two or three times their volume.

1. The night before, place lentils in a large bowl and cover with plenty of water. Add a little salt and allow to soak overnight. If making the same day, soak for at least 4 hours. Change the water a few times if possible.

2. Heat oil in a pot over medium heat. Add onion and salt, cooking 3 to 4 minutes, until onion begins to soften.

3. Add garlic, stir, cook another minute or two.

4. Drain lentils and add to onion mixture along with chili powder, cumin, coriander and oregano. Cook, stirring, until spices are fragrant and lentils are dry, about 1 minute.

5. Add stock or water and bring to a simmer. Reduce heat, cover and simmer over very low heat until lentils are tender, about 20 to 25 minutes.

6. Uncover and cook until lentil mixture thickens, 6 to 8 minutes. Mash with a rubber spatula.

7. Finely chop the chipotle pepper until almost a paste. Combine well with the sour cream and adobo sauce.

8. In a dry skillet, heat each tortilla for 15 seconds on each side just to soften.

9. To assemble tacos, place ¼ cup lentils, 2 tablespoons cheese, 1 tablespoon salsa, ¼ cup lettuce and ½ tablespoon spiced sour cream on each tortilla. Fold over to secure.

Ratatouille | *Paul Denamiel* ~ Serves 2

When Paul Denamiel was asked to teach a DaVinci Master Chef class, he took it as a challenge to create a vegetarian meal that would be just as memorable as his signature meat dishes. He decided to update the French classic ratatouille. "This is a great, colorful way to serve whatever vegetables are in season," says Chef Denamiel. You can cook the vegetables with bacon if you like, or top the dish with a fried or poached egg for extra protein.

4 tablespoons extra-virgin olive
    oil, plus more for finishing
1 clove garlic, minced
1 large beefsteak tomato,
    cored and diced
¼ teaspoon dried oregano
½ teaspoon sugar
Sea salt
Freshly ground black pepper

2 Chinese eggplants, cut into
    ¼-inch-thick rounds
2 small beefsteak tomatoes,
    cored and sliced into
    ¼-inch-thick rounds
2 yellow squash, peeled, seeded and
    sliced into ¼-inch-thick rounds
2 green zucchini, cut in
    ¼-inch-thick rounds

1. Preheat oven to 425 degrees.
2. Start by making a tomato sauce. Place 2 tablespoons of
   the olive oil in a saucepan over medium heat.
3. Add garlic, stirring occasionally, until it is very lightly browned.
4. Add the diced tomato, oregano and sugar, stirring occasionally,
   until tomatoes have softened and begun to stew.
5. Season with salt and pepper
6. Place eggplant, tomato, squash and zucchini in a large bowl and
   drizzle with 2 tablespoons olive oil. Salt, then toss to combine well.
7. When the tomato sauce is done, spread it on the bottom of
   an 8-inch round baking dish with 1-inch-high sides.
8. Arrange the vegetable rounds on top of the
   sauce, either in stacks or layers.
9. Drizzle the vegetables with a little more olive oil, sprinkle with salt and
   place on the middle rack of the oven. Roast for 30 to 40 minutes, or
   until the vegetables are cooked through and have begun to brown
   around the edges. (If you like your ratatouille softer, you can roast an
   additional 20 to 30 minutes, checking for doneness as you go.)

For the ragù:

2¼ cups cooked navy beans, cooking liquid reserved

(see Cesare Casella's basic bean cooking method, at right)

2¼ pounds butternut squash, peeled and seeded

For the glaze:

1½ tablespoons salted butter

4½ teaspoons maple syrup

¾ teaspoon cider vinegar

¾ teaspoon sea salt

¾ teaspoon fresh-ground black pepper

For the kale mixture:

4½ teaspoons extra-virgin olive oil

3 leeks, light green and white parts, well-rinsed, then thinly sliced

2 small cloves garlic, minced

1½ teaspoons fresh rosemary leaves

4½ cups washed and chopped kale leaves, ribs removed

3 tablespoons grated Parmigiano-Reggiano cheese

3 tablespoons roughly chopped dried cranberries

1⅛ teaspoons cider vinegar

Freshly ground black pepper

Pumpkin, Kale and White Bean Ragù | *DNA* ~ Serves 6

"If you want to take care of people using fewer medications and have them be as healthy as possible, you need to take care of the soil where you grow your ingredients and to cook food the right way," says Chef Casella. "You feed the soil and the soil gives back to you." This recipe, adapted from *The New York Times*, is a testament to the rich earth the Thanksgiving Farm staff has cultivated.

1. Cook beans. Keep in cooking liquid until ready to use.
2. Preheat oven to 425 degrees.
3. Cut squash into ½-inch cubes.
4. Combine glaze ingredients in a saucepan over medium heat, stirring until butter melts.
5. Pour glaze over squash and toss to coat evenly.
6. Roast squash in the oven, turning once, until very tender and beginning to brown around the edges, about 30 minutes.
7. Warm olive oil over medium heat. Add leeks, garlic, rosemary and a pinch of salt. Cook, stirring occasionally, until leeks are very soft but not browned, about 15 minutes.
8. Add kale, beans and bean liquid. Simmer for about 10 minutes until kale is tender. Stir in roasted squash followed by the Parmigiano-Reggiano cheese, cranberries, vinegar and ground pepper, to taste. Serve.

Basic Bean
Cooking Method | *Cesare Casella* ~ Makes 6 cups

Thanksgiving Farm grows many varieties of beans, which are rich in magnesium, potassium, phosphorus and other minerals and are a staple in The Center's kitchens. This is the best method for preparing dried beans; the kombu will help them cook faster. "People are sometimes intimidated by cooking beans, but they shouldn't be. It is so simple and you taste the difference when your tooth sinks in," says Chef Casella.

1 pound dried beans
1 tablespoon sea salt
1 onion, quartered
1 carrot, cut in chunks
1 stalk celery, cut in 1-inch pieces
½ head garlic, smashed
½ bay leaf
1½ sprigs fresh rosemary
1½ sprigs fresh thyme
1½ sprigs fresh sage
½ teaspoon whole black peppercorns
5-inch piece kombu seaweed

1. Sort through the beans for dirt and small stones. Wash and drain beans; place in a large bowl and pour in water (depth of water should be twice that of beans). Add the salt and soak overnight.
2. Drain beans and place in a large pot.
3. Tie up the vegetables, herbs and peppercorns in a piece of cheesecloth.
4. Put beans, cheesecloth bundle, kombu and 8 cups water in a large pot over medium heat and bring to a low boil.
5. Lower to a simmer and cook until the beans are tender but not falling apart. You may need to add more water as they cook. Skim foam off as it collects on the surface. Start checking beans for doneness after 1 hour.
6. Cool beans in cooking liquid to absorb more flavor, then remove herb bundle and seaweed.

Cooking Beans With Kombu

When the residential chefs make bean dishes, they cook the beans beforehand with kombu, an edible kelp that is popular in East Asia and is a rich source of dietary fiber. Soaking and cooking with kombu aids in the digestion of beans by removing phytic acid and lectins. Kombu also cuts down on the cooking time for the beans, softens them, and adds a delicious, meaty flavor. It is mineral-rich with calcium, iodine, magnesium, iron and folate.

Cauliflower Pizza | *DNA* ~ Serves 4

For the "crust":

1¼ pounds frozen
cauliflower florets

3 tablespoons extra-
virgin olive oil

4 large eggs

¾ teaspoon dried oregano

1½ teaspoons minced garlic

¾ teaspoon granulated
garlic

1¼ teaspoons sea salt

¼ teaspoon fresh-ground
black pepper

3 cups grated
mozzarella cheese

For the topping:

1 cup pommarola (see
page 60) or other
tomato sauce

1 cup grated mozzarella
cheese

vegetables or pepperoni,
as desired

This past year, DNA has been working to reduce grain-based carbohydrates in the menus. The kitchen also freezes a lot of cauliflower in the fall to extend the farm's bounty into the winter. This wheatless recipe delivers the new nutritional goal, uses The Center's robust cauliflower crop, and mimics an all-time favorite of guests and staff: pizza.

1. Place the cauliflower florets in a food processor and pulse until they look like grains of rice. Do not overpulse or you will end up with a puree.
2. Place the riced cauliflower in a microwave-safe bowl, cover with plastic wrap and microwave for about 6 minutes. There is no need to add water, as the natural moisture in the cauliflower is enough to cook it. Allow cauliflower to cool.
3. Preheat oven to 450 degrees.
4. Trace four 7-inch circles on a piece of parchment paper lining a sheet pan. Turn over the parchment and, using the circles as guides, oil the areas where your individual pizzas will go.
5. In a medium bowl, whisk the eggs, oregano, minced garlic, granulated garlic, salt and pepper.
6. Add the cooled cauliflower and the mozzarella. Stir thoroughly to combine ingredients.
7. Use a 1-cup measure to scoop up batter and transfer to oiled parchment. Flatten each to make a thin, even layer on each of the 4 circles.
8. Place sheet pan in the oven and bake for 15 minutes. This is the "shell" and can be done ahead.
9. Top each 7-inch round with ¼ cup tomato sauce, ¼ cup grated mozzarella cheese and any vegetables or pepperoni, if desired. Raise the temperature of the oven to 500 degrees and bake (or place under a broiler at high heat) just until cheese is melted (about 3 to 4 minutes).

FEEDING *the* HEART | 71

CHAPTER FOUR

The Barnyard

Five-Oh-Two is standing alone. She is in an open field at Stonewall Preserve, gazing at the horizon. Her doleful brown eyes are the size of honey jars and her coat is a creamy white flecked with chocolate. She is Italian, a Chianina, a breed of cattle that dates to Roman times and is the source of the famed bistecca Fiorentina. At Thanksgiving Farm, 502 is one of more than 50 head of cattle, and by far the oldest. She is also the favorite at the farm, more loved than any of the Black Angus or Devon that produce much of the beef used by The Center's kitchens.

The sole remaining member of a herd The Center began to build two decades ago, 502 is a living legacy of president and CEO Patrick Dollard's early vision for an agricultural program that would connect residents, students, staff and the Hurleyville community through farming.

Thanksgiving Farm's first animals were three draft horses used to drive large wagons for farm tours and pull some basic farm implements for working the fields. They were part of Dollard's plan to provide meaningful training and work for residents and help The Center begin producing its own food. At the time The Center owned a single 50-acre farm and had just rented another 15 acres for four years. Two Irish Dexter cows arrived in 1995; after the Dexters came the bees, then several goats, a few chickens, and in 1997, five Shetland sheep. In the early 2000s, when 502 arrived, she was one of a small herd The Center had begun to assemble with Chef Cesare Casella, today the head of the Department of Nourishment Arts, or DNA.

"We created our first CSA in 1993, but we wanted to take it to the next level," says Dollard. "I thought it would be cool to grow food and get people from the community to come and get involved in The Center." When Dollard met resistance from some who were unwilling to work with people with disabilities, he was angered but unfazed and set out to create the farm he wanted. "It was more

Beef & Lamb

Pork

(Poultry directory on next page)

me being angry and saying I'll do it myself. I started by getting the best farmers. Then I met Cesare and it changed my life."

At the time, Chef Casella was looking to board six Chianina he was raising to supply steak for his New York City restaurant, Beppe. He was introduced to The Center simply as a place to keep his cattle, and met Dollard in the process. But in the decade that followed, Dollard and Casella started collaborating on other farm projects and an unexpected partnership developed. Thanksgiving Farm began to take shape as Dollard had envisioned, with both the livestock and crop programs growing and thriving. Today the farm continues to expand and food production is critical to The Center's work.

With some 130 pigs, 40 head of cattle and 900 laying hens, the farm plays a key role in providing the highest-quality humanely raised pork, beef and eggs for DNA kitchens. The animals also play an increasingly important role in The Center's living classrooms, which expose students to various aspects of animal husbandry: watering cattle, forking hay, herding sheep, collecting compost, inspecting fencing.

For Dollard it is a life come full-circle. "I grew up on a farm, but I was too small to pitch hay or drive a wagon, so my grandfather taught me to drive the horses around," he says. "I had this romantic notion about farmers. I know how hard it is to work with disabilities. I always wanted to combine working the land and fields and caring for people."

Beef & Lamb

Farmer's Pasture-Raised Beef Chili and Summer Tomatoes | *DNA* ~ Serves 5

Chili is a one-pot meal that provides protein, vegetables and complex carbohydrates. Serve it with garnishes in separate bowls so people can choose: Sour cream, grated sharp cheddar, pickled jalapeños, diced red onion, fresh cilantro and lime wedges are a few of the favorites at The Center.

1½ cups cooked beans with their liquid (kidney, garbanzo, or a mixture of your choice)
2¼ tablespoons extra-virgin oil
1¼ pounds pasture-raised ground beef
1¼ cups diced onion

⅓ cup finely chopped celery
1 teaspoon minced garlic
⅔ cup diced red bell pepper
⅓ teaspoon freshly ground black pepper (or more to taste)
1¼ tablespoons chili powder
⅔ teaspoon paprika
1¼ teaspoons dried oregano
⅔ teaspoon granulated onion

2 teaspoons ground cumin
2 teaspoons ground coriander
1¼ tablespoons cocoa powder
1¼ tablespoons tomato paste
2 cups whole peeled canned tomatoes with juice
1¼ cups beef stock
½ cup brewed decaffeinated coffee
2 teaspoons sea salt

1. Prepare beans according to directions, or use canned beans. If making your own, allow them to cool in their cooking liquid (do not drain).
2. Pour the olive oil into a soup pot and add the beef. Cook over medium heat until the meat is browned. Transfer the meat to a separate bowl with a slotted spoon.
3. Add the onion, celery, garlic and bell pepper, and sauté over medium heat, stirring occasionally, until the vegetables begin to soften.
4. Push the vegetables to one side of the pot with a wooden spoon. On the cleared spot add the black pepper, chili powder, paprika, oregano, granulated onion, cumin, coriander and cocoa, allowing the mixture to toast lightly. Stir the spices into the vegetables. Add the tomato paste, stir and cook briefly.
5. Crush the tomatoes with your hands or pulse briefly in a food processor. Add tomatoes and their juice to the pot, followed by the beef stock and coffee.
6. Stir in the browned beef and simmer, covered, for 1 to 1½ hours.
7. Add the beans and their cooking liquid. Simmer another 20 minutes.
8. Taste, correcting for seasoning, and serve.

Good-for-You Bone Broth

DNA ~ Yield: 2½ gallons

Stocks made with bones contain nutrients that are key to healing, especially for individuals with gastrointestinal or bone problems. Freeze this stock in quart containers and use to make soups, risotto, for saucing and braising.

1. Preheat oven to 425 degrees.
2. Place the bones on a sheet pan and roast until well browned, about an hour. Turn once during cooking.
3. Reserving the sheet pan with its fat, transfer the bones to a stock pot and add the water; bring to a simmer. Skim off any scum that rises to the surface.
4. Toss the vegetables in the fat from the roasting pan. Drain excess fat.
5. Reduce oven temperature to 400 degrees and roast the vegetables until browned, about 40 minutes. Stir in the tomato paste to coat vegetables; roast another 10 minutes. Transfer vegetables to a bowl and set aside. Deglaze the roasting pan with wine and add to the stock.
6. Simmer the stock for 4 hours. Add the roasted vegetables, salt, peppercorns and bay leaves. Return to a simmer and cook 2 to 8 hours longer.
7. Line a strainer with cheesecloth and strain stock into storage containers; refrigerate.
8. When stock is cold, remove the fat that has collected on top (use reserved fat for cooking, if desired). You can use immediately or freeze for up to 6 months.

20 pounds bones
    from pasture-raised beef
3 gallons cold water
1 cup tomato paste
4 cups quartered onions
2 cups celeriac, peeled and cut in chunks, or celery
2 cups carrot, peeled and cut in chunks
½ cup red or white wine
2 tablespoons sea salt
¾ tablespoon whole black peppercorns
3 dried bay leaves, broken in two

Fennel-Studded Meatloaf with Summer Herbs | *DNA* ~ Serves 6

"I start with what we can grow in the Northeast," says Chef Parten. "I'm not going to make something with pineapple. Eating seasonally and locally is a way to eat healthy. We are not concerned with the newest dish or the most exotic from far away. We want quality, and that is what we have. It is connected to the land."

2 tablespoons extra-virgin olive oil
¾ cup finely chopped spring onion
2 cloves garlic, minced
¾ cup finely diced fennel bulb
½ cup peeled grated broccoli stalk
1 cup grated turnip
2 pounds 90-percent-lean ground beef
7 tablespoons tomato paste
1 cup cooked brown basmati rice
2 large eggs, slightly beaten
1 tablespoon Worcestershire sauce
1 tablespoon minced fresh thyme leaves
1 tablespoon chopped garlic chives
1 teaspoon salt
1½ teaspoons dry mustard
¼ teaspoon freshly ground black pepper
Ketchup

1. Preheat the oven to 350 degrees.
2. Place the olive oil in a sauté pan with the spring onion, garlic, fennel, broccoli stalk and turnip. Heat over medium until the vegetables are soft but not browned. Remove from heat and let cool.
3. In a large bowl, combine the cooled cooked vegetables with the ground beef, tomato paste, rice, egg, Worcestershire sauce, thyme, garlic chives, dry mustard, salt and pepper. Mix lightly but thoroughly.
4. Shape the mixture into a loaf measuring approximately 9 by 4 by 3 inches. Place on a foil-lined baking sheet and top with ketchup. Bake in a 350-degree oven for 45 minutes to an hour, or until juices run clear. Cut loaf into 6 equal portions approximately 1½ inches thick.

Barnyard Chores

✔ **Compost pickup for pigs:** Once a day, pick up compost at from kitchen locations for pig feeding

✔ **Clean compost bins:** Once a day, scrub empty compost bins before returning to kitchen

✔ **Pig bedding:** Three times a week, fork hay and straw into pig pens for bedding

✔ **Chicken bedding:** Three times a week, spread out hay and straw for bedding in chicken polyhouse

✔ **Cow bedding:** Three times a week, roll out round bale and spread for cow bedding

✔ **Cow feed and water:** Once a day, pitch hay into feed troughs for cows; use hose to fill water troughs

✔ **Fence inspection:** Once a day, inspect fencing for wire damage or broken posts

✔ **Herd sheep:** Once or twice a week, help farmers move sheep from pasture to pasture

Dairy

The Milk Train

While Thanksgiving Farm does not yet have a herd of dairy cows or goats, Hurleyville and the land around The Center for Discovery have a deep connection to milk production.

In the years after Sullivan County was founded, in 1809, immigrants and city dwellers began moving to the area for the fresh air, idyllic rural setting and the promise of a new life. By the 1850s, even though the soil was rocky and crop cultivation a challenge, thousands of small farms had sprung up, with families growing food for their own consumption.

At the time, dairy cows were a rarity because they were expensive to keep, but that changed with the arrival of the railroad in 1870. Suddenly there was a market for milk in New York City and farmers were quick to meet the demand. Over the next decade, a thriving industry developed, and by 1890 there were some 4,000 local farms, most of which kept milk cows. Soon Sullivan County was shipping out nine to ten million cans of

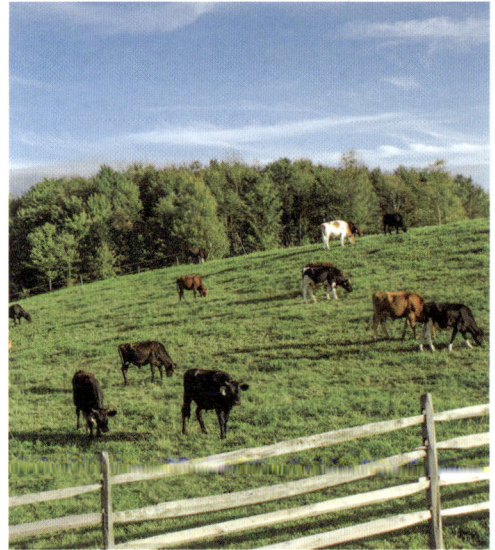

milk a year on the Ontario & Western Railway (O&W). By 1940 the area counted 26,000 dairy cows. Next to tourism, milk was Sullivan County's main industry, according to John Conway, the official county historian, who also works at The Center.

The majority of the cows were Holstein-Friesians, which were economical to keep and produced a high volume of milk, says Conway. Creameries too began to flourish, producing butter and farmer's cheese. The industry, though, quickly began to decline once the O&W stopped running and there was no longer an efficient way to get fresh milk to New Yorkers. Land became more valuable for resorts like Grossinger's and bungalow colony getaways.

Today, Sullivan County once again has a handful of dairy farms and The Center is nurturing an agricultural revival in the area by working with the Open Space Institute, a non-profit dedicated to the preservation of scenic and historic landscapes. Through OSI, The Center has been able to re-establish Stonewall Preserve, one of the region's oldest farms, and protect it with an agricultural easement. The two organizations have also partnered to create Tutto Bene Farm, a 132-acre parcel of land where fruit and herbs are grown, and Sweet Hill Farm, a 162-acre spread where young adults with autism will raise goats and tap trees for maple syrup.

In their latest initiative, The Center and OSI are working to convert nine miles of the old O&W rail line into parkland. The Milk Train RailTrail is being developed as a hiking/biking trail to be used by residents, their families, locals and tourists, once again tying The Center to Sullivan County's dairy traditions.

Power Smoothie | *DNA* ~ Serves 4

. . . .

Traditional smoothies are very high in sugar, but DNA's special recipe is chock-full of protein, according to assistant chief of DNA Jennifer Franck.

2 large eggs
2 cups plain whole-milk Greek yogurt
2 peeled bananas
½ cup whole milk
1 teaspoon vanilla extract
2 tablespoons honey

1. Bring the eggs to room temperature. This will keep them from cracking.
2. Bring a pot of water to a boil. Carefully add the eggs and return the water to a simmer. Cook for about 5 minutes, until eggs are soft-boiled.
3. Remove and cool under running water. Crack the shells and run under cool water again. Peel and place in the blender.
4. Add the remaining ingredients and blend until smooth. You may have to do this in two batches, depending on the capacity of the blender jar. Serve.

Lamb and Beef Kebabs with Yogurt, Coriander and Mint | *Maria Loi* ~ Serves 8

This is a quintessentially Greek recipe that DaVinci Master Chef Maria Loi wanted to share with DNA chefs because it is easily adapted to the cuisines of various countries and is easy to cook, serve, and eat. "The flavors of the Mediterranean are often considered when cooking, but not always adhered to," says Chef Loi. "As a Greek chef, I take great pride in my heritage and my food, so I wanted to share the flavors of my country and my life with the staff, knowing that they would translate it into something the residents would love."

2 onions, peeled and quartered
1 pound ground lamb
1 pound ground beef
1 egg, beaten
½ teaspoon minced fresh oregano
½ teaspoon minced fresh mint
½ teaspoon ground coriander
½ teaspoon ground cumin
2 teaspoons sea salt
½ teaspoon freshly ground
   black pepper

¼ cup extra-virgin olive oil
8 slices whole wheat pita
1 pound low-fat Greek yogurt
3 cloves garlic, finely grated
2 teaspoons fresh chopped dill
1 teaspoon crushed red
   pepper flakes (optional)
Leaves from ½ bunch fresh
   Italian parsley

1. Preheat the oven to 400 degrees.
2. Place the onion in a blender and puree until smooth.
3. Transfer the puree to a large bowl. Stir in the ground lamb and beef, egg, oregano, mint, coriander, cumin, salt and pepper and mix well.
4. Using a #12 scoop (⅓ cup), form the mixture into oval patties.
5. Brush the kebabs with olive oil. Place in oven to bake for 10 to 15 minutes, turning for even browning.
6. While the kebabs are cooking, make the sauce by mixing the yogurt, grated garlic and dill in a bowl until well-blended.
7. Remove the kebabs from the oven.
8. Lay a pita on a plate and spread with 2 to 3 tablespoons of the yogurt mixture. Place a kebab on top and sprinkle with a pinch of crushed red pepper, if using. Garnish with parsley leaves. Serve.

Lamb-Farro Soup with Tuscan Black Kale | *Pecko Zantilaveevan* ~ Serves 6

Pecko Zantilaveevan of The Four Seasons restaurant in New York City shared a rustic, restorative soup with DNA chefs. "As children, our mothers have all made us soup, and there's a sort of comfort that comes to mind when I reminisce about having my mother's soup as a child. I wanted to re-create that sort of comfort at The Center and found the perfect ingredients there." Chef Casella likes finishing each bowl of this soup Tuscan-style—with a swirl of olive oil.

1. Place the stock in a large soup pot over high heat. Bring to a boil, then reduce to a simmer. While the stock is simmering, prep ingredients as specified at right: Dice the lamb and vegetables, slice the garlic, chop the herbs.

2. When the stock has simmered for a few minutes, turn up the heat and add the farro.

3. Place olive oil in a large skillet over medium-high heat and add the diced lamb. When it is well-browned, season lightly with salt, white pepper and red pepper flakes. Drain off excess fat and add the meat to the soup pot. Return soup to a simmer.

4. Pour the olive oil into a large sauté pan. Add the onions and leek and cook over medium heat for 3 to 4 minutes. Add the sliced garlic and continue to sauté for another 3 minutes; add carrots, then celery and kale. When the vegetables are soft, season lightly with salt and pepper and add to the stock pot.

5. Let the soup cook for about 30 minutes at a simmer until the broth is well-infused with lamb flavor and the other flavors have had a chance to develop and meld.

6. To serve, stir in the chopped herbs and lemon zest, then taste for seasoning. (If not serving at once, allow the soup to cool completely at this point, then refrigerate.)

7. Divide the soup equally among 6 bowls, and finish each with the shaved Parmigiano and a swirl of extra-virgin olive oil.

2 quarts lamb stock (if not available, use chicken stock)

4 ounces uncooked farro

1 pound lamb shoulder, trimmed of excess fat and diced into ¼-inch cubes

Sea salt

Ground white pepper

1 teaspoon crushed red pepper flakes

2 tablespoons extra-virgin olive oil, plus additional olive oil for finishing

1 small onion, diced

1 leek, white and light green parts only, halved, rinsed and diced

5 cloves garlic, sliced thin

1 carrot, diced

2 stalks celery, diced

1 pound Tuscan black kale, stems removed and cut into bite-sized pieces

1 teaspoon fresh rosemary needles, blanched and chopped

1 teaspoon chopped fresh thyme leaves

2 tablespoons chopped fresh Italian parsley

1 tablespoon blanched and minced lemon zest

6 ounces shaved Parmigiano-Reggiano cheese

The Conversation
Breeding Pigs

DNA chief Cesare Casella and head herdsman Brett Budde discuss a special breed.

Cesare Casella: *I remember when we started out with the pigs, was it 12 years ago? I wanted to import the Cinta Senese, an ancient Tuscan pig you see in frescoes back to the Renaissance. But we weren't allowed to.*

Brett Budde: *Instead we started cross-breeding to make an animal specific to our needs—Durocs, Tamworths, Berkshires, English Large Blacks. We wanted pigs that would do well outside, that are good tempered.*

CC: *What you get is a wonderful flavor of a pig that people used to eat 60 or more years ago. Sullivan County is fantastic for pigs.*

BB: *Historically this is where Jewish families came to escape New York City, so there hasn't been a tradition of raising pigs here. But you're right, the land here is perfect for them. It's rocky and muddy and rutty.*

CC: *We also use the pigs to increase the fertility of the fields.*

BB: *You know the field where we kept the pigs year before last? Greg planted buckwheat there and it grew to be three-and-a-half feet tall. The bees were in it like crazy. The field would hum.*

CC: *It is an organic environment. Everything hums.*

Pork

On-The-Fly Moussaka | *April Bloomfield* ~ Serves 12

When Spotted Pig chef April Bloomfield was asked to teach a DaVinci Master Chef class, she thought of the Greek dish moussaka because it was something she had always wanted to try herself. "I came up with a recipe that was fun for me to make and good for the staff to make alongside me, and good to eat," she says. To Bloomfield, The Center's work with the medically fragile was an eye-opener. "It is really inspiring that they are taking the time to help nurture each person on an individual level."

5 eggplants, sliced
    ¼-inch thick
Sea salt to draw moisture
    out of eggplant
½ cup extra-virgin olive oil
3 tablespoons salted butter
2 onions, finely chopped
4 stalks celery, finely chopped
1 carrot, finely chopped
5 cloves garlic, sliced

1½ pounds ground pork (or
    substitute ground lamb)
1 pound ground beef
¼ pound pancetta, minced
½ cup whole milk
16 ounces canned crushed plum
    tomatoes, including the juice
1 cup white wine
2 tablespoons freshly ground
    black pepper

3 tablespoons sea salt
1 cup grated Parmigiano-
    Reggiano cheese

For the béchamel sauce:
5 tablespoons butter
4 tablespoons flour
3 cups whole milk
2 teaspoons salt
½ teaspoon ground nutmeg

1. Lay the eggplant slices on a tray and salt liberally on both sides. Set aside.
2. In a 6- to 8-quart heavy-bottomed saucepan, heat ¼ cup olive oil and butter over a medium flame. Add the onion, celery, carrot and garlic and sweat until vegetables are translucent.
3. Add pork (or lamb), beef and pancetta to the vegetables. Brown over high heat, stirring constantly, for about 15 to 20 minutes.
4. Pour in the milk and simmer until almost dry, about 10 minutes.
5. Add the tomatoes and simmer for an additional 15 minutes.
6. Add the wine and briefly bring to a boil, then reduce heat. Simmer the ragù for 2 to 2½ hours to meld flavors. Season to taste.
7. Pat the eggplant dry. In a sauté pan, heat the remaining quarter cup of oil over medium-high and add the eggplant. Sauté for 2 to 3 minutes per side until golden brown. Transfer to paper towels to drain.

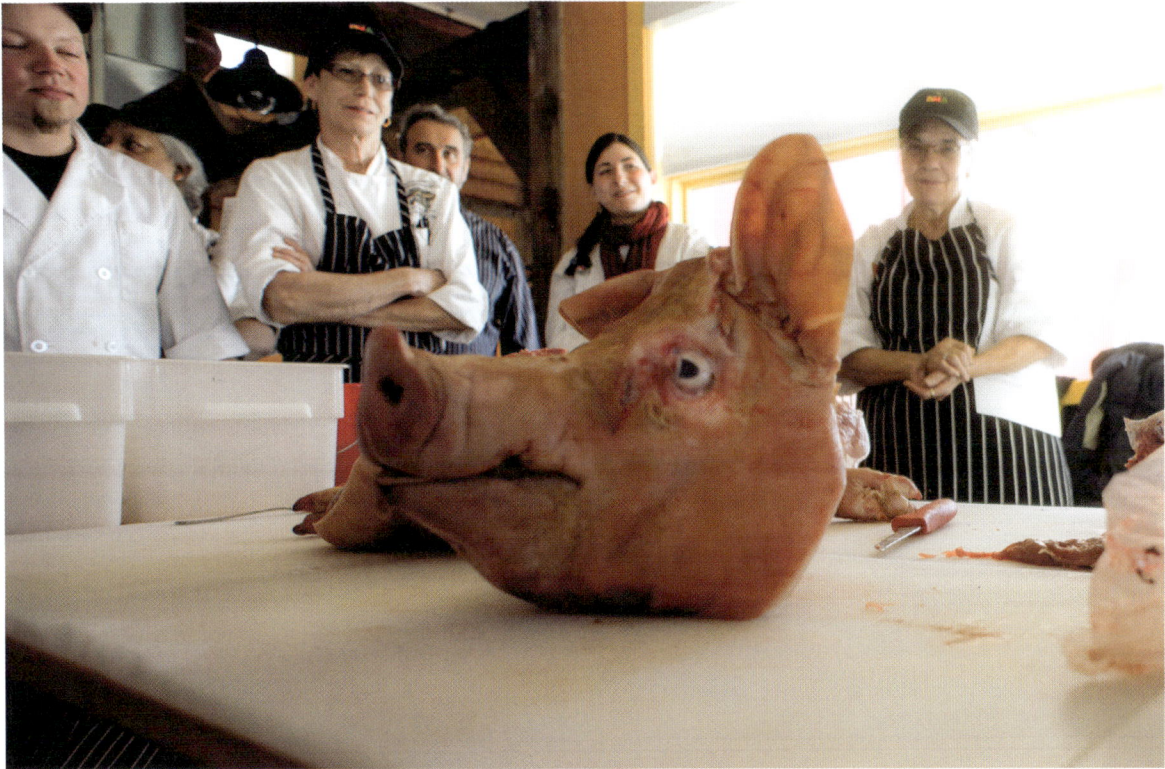

Make the béchamel:

1. In a medium saucepan, make a roux: Heat the butter over a medium-low burner until it melts, then gradually add flour and stir until smooth.

2. Continue cooking over medium-low heat, stirring constantly, until the mixture turns a sandy color, about 6 to 7 minutes.

3. In a separate pan, heat the milk almost to the boiling point. Add the hot milk to the butter mixture one cup at a time, whisking continuously to avoid lumps.

4. Bring the mixture to a low boil and cook 10 minutes, stirring continually, then remove from heat. Season with salt and nutmeg, and set aside until ready to use.

To assemble:

1. Preheat the oven to 375 degrees.

2. Remember, you are basically making a lasagna. Oil a 9-by-13-inch casserole dish and spread the bottom with a layer of ragù. Follow with a sprinkling of grated Parmigiano, a layer of eggplant, a layer of béchamel and then another of ragù. Repeat until it reaches the top of the dish.

3. The final layer should be eggplant with béchamel over it. Finish with remaining Parmigiano and bake for 45 minutes to 1 hour, or until golden and bubbly.

4. Remove and cool for at least 30 minutes to make sure the moussaka is completely set. You can serve with a final dusting of Parmigiano cheese.

Pork and Ginger Pot Stickers

DNA ~ Yield: about 60 pot stickers

. . . .

This special-occasion dish might be a little labor-intensive, but it's well worth the effort. "They will be gone in minutes," predicts Chef Parten.

4 cups finely chopped
 green cabbage
1 tablespoon sea salt
½ pound ground pork
2 tablespoons grated
 peeled fresh gingerroot
3 tablespoons
 minced garlic
4 tablespoons tamari
2 tablespoons toasted
 sesame oil
1 large egg
60 wonton wrappers
2 tablespoons oil
 or pork fat
Water

For the filling:

1. Combine the cabbage and half the salt in a large bowl. Toss, then set aside for 30 minutes.
2. Transfer cabbage to a clean dish towel or doubled piece of cheesecloth. Gather the ends together and twist to squeeze out as much moisture as possible from the cabbage.
3. In a separate bowl, combine the wrung-dry cabbage with the pork, ginger, garlic, tamari, sesame oil, egg, and the remaining ½ tablespoon salt. Mix thoroughly.

Assembling the pot stickers:

1. Lay a few wrappers on your cutting board, covering the remainder with a damp dish towel so they do not dry out. Brush half the perimeter of each square with water, then place about ½ tablespoon of the filling in the center. Avoid getting filling on the edges of the wrappers—it will prevent them from sealing properly.
2. Fold each wrapper in half so the edges meet. Seal each dumpling by pressing the wrapper edges between your fingers. Position the dumpling with the seal pointing up (not lying on its side). Starting at the center, fold a small piece of the edge to form a pleat. Repeat, working toward the bottom right corner, so that each dumpling has two or three pleats. Then duplicate these steps, starting at the center and working toward the bottom left corner. Gently press the dumplings onto the work surface to flatten the bottoms. Continue filling and folding wrappers in this way until all the filling has been used.

3. Heat the oil or pork fat in a nonstick skillet over high heat. Swirl to coat the pan.

4. When the oil or fat begins to shimmer, add the pot stickers, flattened bottoms down. Turn the flame down to medium.

5. Cook, undisturbed, until lightly browned on the bottom, about 4 minutes. Watch carefully, as they can brown quickly.

6. Add about ½ cup of water and immediately cover to prevent the pot stickers from splitting. Steam until the dumplings are puffy yet firm and water has evaporated, 5 to 6 minutes. Check from time to time to make sure skillet has not boiled dry before pot stickers are done.

7. After water has evaporated, remove the lid and continue to cook over medium-high heat to recrisp the pot stickers on the bottom, 2 to 3 minutes. Transfer to a platter and serve with an Asian-style dipping sauce.

The Conversation
Connecting Farming to Therapy

Director of speech therapy Maria Landon, speech therapist Kristina Carraccia, occupational therapist Coleen Visconti and Nicole Kinney, head of clinical services, discuss their work and the farm.

Kristina Carraccia: *If the residents are sorting vegetables in the washbarn, they don't have to eat those vegetables. They benefit from just being around the food; they don't have to eat it.*

Coleen Visconti: *A couple of weeks ago, radishes and chives were in season. So some of the residents helped harvest the vegetables and made farmer's cream cheese spread. They got to prepare it and taste it if they wanted. It's real.*

KC: *Farm work can be vigorous, and that activity helps the brain. It's not just getting the wiggles out. It's to turn on the brain for learning.*

CV: *If you are screwing on the cap of a honey bottle you are working on fine motor skills. If you are bending down, you are working on flexibility. Doing heavy work helps self-regulate, to pace yourself, to participate in school days.*

Maria Landon: *When we are out in the fields, we work on things like how to ask a question. So many of our students are skilled at answering a question, but asking one is more complicated.*

Nicole Kinney: *To work on a farm in a group setting you need teamwork, and communication is hugely important.*

ML: *It is helping students come out of their bubble.*

The Pigs

One of the favorite barnyard activities for students is helping to feed the farm's herd of pigs. After collecting leftover vegetables (no table scraps!) from one of the kitchens on campus, participants get to feed and interact with the animals, who are well-socialized from the time they are small. Specially designed feeding stations ensure that chore time is a safe and clean experience. "Everyone is right there," says Brett Budde, the head herdsman. "There is a feed trough and a bunch of pigs and a bunch of residents. They can reach out and touch each other."

Each student, of course, reacts differently. Some find it relaxing to be around the animals, others might be a little nervous. "Others just want to talk about when they'll become meat," adds Budde.

Sullivan County Pork Ribs with Rosemary | *Cesare Casella* ~ Serves 6

"I use the ingredients from upstate New York to make a traditional dish I used to cook in Lucca," says Chef Casella. "The basis of Italian cooking is using good ingredients. That's what we have at the Center." The secret to this recipe: marinating the ribs for two days before cooking.

2 pounds St. Louis-style pork spareribs, cut into individual ribs
½ teaspoon sea salt
¼ teaspoon freshly ground black pepper
2 teaspoons garam masala
¼ cup extra-virgin olive oil
2 cloves garlic, roughly chopped
2 tablespoons roughly chopped rosemary
¼ cup white wine
¾ pound fresh ripe tomatoes, roughly chopped

Preparation:
Two days before cooking, rub the ribs with salt and pepper, garam masala, and half the olive oil. Cover with plastic wrap and keep refrigerated.

To cook:
1. Preheat the oven to 350 degrees.
2. Place the ribs on a roasting pan and bake for 20 minutes. Sprinkle with the remaining 2 tablespoons olive oil, garlic and rosemary. Stir to coat.
3. Bake until garlic begins to soften, about 20 minutes.
4. Add wine and return to oven. When wine has evaporated, after about 20 more minutes, turn the ribs and add the tomatoes.
5. Taste and adjust seasoning with salt and pepper. Roast ribs for another 25 minutes, using the juices to baste.
6. Transfer the ribs to a platter and serve.

Easy Summer Pork and Vegetable Stew | *Paul Denamiel* ~ Serves 4

French-born DaVinci Master Chef Paul Denamiel chose to make this stew based on what was fresh when he visited Thanksgiving Farm. It is the sort of one-pot dish he ate as a young boy, he says. "That's the way my grandparents cooked and the way I grew up. I try to use what's local and seasonal, for both vegetables and herbs," he adds. "Stew is great for any season, and good hot or cold."

Denamiel also thought the stew would fit easily into DNA's seasonal menu rotation. "The fact that so much is grown on-site is amazing, and the access to local seasonal ingredients is a great way for everyone to eat. It's also so amazing to see how the food program is modified to meet the special needs of so many people, to target their specific nutritional requirements. The food also tastes great, which is a nice change from some facilities that prepare boring, bland food."

1 tablespoon extra-virgin olive oil
¼ pound minced bacon
½ pound pork stew meat
1 medium onion, finely diced
2 large carrots, diced
1 yellow bell pepper, seeded and sliced
2 cloves garlic, minced
½ cup sherry
1 large zucchini, diced

28-ounce can peeled whole tomatoes, with juice
2½ cups water
1 tablespoon chopped fresh basil
1 teaspoon chopped fresh oregano
1 teaspoon chopped fresh parsley
Salt
Freshly ground black pepper
15 ounces haricots verts, cut in 1-inch lengths

1. Heat olive oil in a large pot over medium heat. Add the bacon and cook until translucent, about 8 minutes.
2. Add the pork, onion, carrots, bell pepper and garlic. Cook for 10 minutes over medium heat, stirring often, until carrots are slightly tender.
3. Add the sherry and stir until it evaporates.
4. Stir in the zucchini. Add the tomatoes and their juice, then the water. Season with basil, oregano, parsley, salt and pepper. Bring to a boil. Reduce to low and let simmer for 40 minutes.
5. Stir haricots verts into pot and cook for an additional 5 minutes.
6. Serve the stew on its own or over rice or quinoa.

Fresh Corn Tamales, Pork Carnitas and Chile Mecco Sauce | *Sue Torres* ~ Yield: 20 tamales

Corn was in season when DaVinci Master Chef Sue Torres visited The Center. Known for her Mexican cuisine, Torres immediately thought of tamales. The chile used in this dish, chile mecco, is a dried smoked jalapeño specific to the Tabasco region. "The chile mecco's smoky flavor reminds me of a summertime barbeque and it pairs beautifully with sweet corn," Torres says.

"The recipe is flavorful, fun and adaptable," she continues. "I thought the chefs at DNA would enjoy making it with me and add their own twist to it eventually." This multilayered recipe is among the more ambitious dishes demonstrated by the DaVinci Master Chefs during their seminars. At home you might want to watch a video on tamale making as a guide, and prepare the chile mecco sauce a day ahead.

For the fresh corn tamales:

6 cups fresh corn kernels, from 10 to 12
    ears sweet corn, husks reserved
Milk from the cobs
2 teaspoons sea salt
3 tablespoons sugar (or honey, if you prefer)
4 tablespoons unsalted butter, at room temperature
4 tablespoons crème fraîche or sour cream
1¼ cups corn flour

Prepare the corn filling:

1. Shuck the corn. Place husks in a bowl of room-temperature water and soak for 10 minutes to make them pliable.
2. Cut the kernels off the cobs into a bowl.
3. Hold each cob over the bowl and, pressing down and using a scraping motion, use the back of a knife to extract the milk from each cob.
4. Now make the corn dough (depending on the size of your food processor, you may have to do this in 2 batches).

5. Put half the corn kernels and the milk in a food processor and pulse for about 3 minutes.
6. Add the remaining ingredients (if corn is supersweet, you can use much less sugar or honey) and puree for another 3 minutes. Taste and season with additional salt if needed. Transfer the dough to a bowl.

Assemble and cook the tamales:

1. Use the leaves from the largest husks for the tamale wrappers. Position 2 leaves vertically side by side and overlapping, tapered ends facing away. The wrapper should be about 4 to 5 inches wide.
2. Scoop 2 heaping tablespoons of corn dough into the center of each. Fold the right and left sides over the dough, followed by the top and bottom. Seal with plastic wrap. Repeat until all the dough is used up.
3. Arrange a terry cloth towel in a steamer basket, then line the bottom and sides with the leftover leaves from the husks.
4. Lay the tamales side by side in the steamer and fold the leaves and terry cloth over them. Cook 15 to 20 minutes.

5. To test for doneness, remove a tamale from the steamer. Undo the plastic wrap and unfold the husk: the dough inside should be firm and set. If it's ready, remove the remaining tamales from the steamer and remove plastic wrap.

Tip when steaming: To avoid smoking your tamales, put a penny in the water before heating it. If the pan begins to boil dry you'll be alerted by the rattling of the penny.

For the pork carnitas:

This recipe can be made in advance; you also get improved flavor if the carnitas sits for a day.

1 cup fresh-squeezed orange juice
¼ cup fresh-squeezed lime juice
1 teaspoon dried oregano
½ cup white vinegar
5 guajillo chiles, cleaned and seeds removed
5 ancho chiles, cleaned and seeds removed
3 chile de arbol, cleaned and seeds removed
1 tablespoon ground coriander
1 teaspoon ground cumin
1 cup diced red onion
6 cloves garlic
2 tablespoons sea salt
4 pounds pork shoulder, cut into 1½-inch cubes

1. Puree all ingredients except the pork shoulder in the blender.
2. Place the pork in a heavy-bottomed rondeau pan, then add the puree. There should be enough liquid to cover the pork.

3. Bring to a simmer and cook over medium heat until tender, about 2 hours, checking occasionally. If the carnitas seems to be drying out, add more water.

For the chile mecco sauce:

6 to 7 chile mecco (order online or substitute chipotle chiles)
6 cups roasted tomatoes
1 cup roasted onions
½ cup roasted garlic
2 tablespoons olive oil
Salt

1. Preheat the oven to 350 degrees.
2. Toast chile mecco peppers for two minutes; turn and repeat.
3. Bring 1 quart of water to a boil. Add the toasted chile mecco to the water and lower the heat to medium. Cook for 30 to 40 minutes, until the thick skins are tender.
4. In a blender, puree tomatoes and their cooking juice with the peeled roast onion, roast garlic paste and chile mecco. Add salt, to taste.
5. Heat the oil in a heavy-bottomed pot. Add the puree. Bring to a boil, then reduce heat and cook 5 minutes. Season with salt.
6. To serve, place a tamale on a plate with some carnitas. Serve the sauce in a separate dish or spoon a little beside each tamale.

Poultry

Mandarin Chicken Salad with Sesame-Ginger Dressing | *DNA* ~ Serves 6

DNA's inspirations are wide-ranging. This salad, a riff on a favorite entree at a well-known fast-food chain, helps reluctant eaters realize that healthy and delicious don't have to be mutually exclusive. It is a homey meal, popular with staff and residents alike. The candied almonds are made with Thanksgiving Farm honey; the tamari contains little sodium and is wheat-free. For a milder version, feel free to omit the cayenne in the dressing.

For the candied nuts:

2 tablespoons honey
1 tablespoon sunflower oil
½ cup sliced almonds

1. Preheat the oven to 350 degrees.
2. In a bowl, whisk the honey and oil until thoroughly emulsified. Toss with almonds and scatter on a parchment-lined or lightly oiled baking sheet. Toast 10 minutes, until mixture is golden and bubbling. Allow to cool until hardened, then break into pieces. Set aside.

For the sesame-ginger dressing:

Yield: 1½ cups
¼ cup sesame seeds
2 teaspoons minced garlic
1 teaspoon finely grated peeled fresh gingerroot
¼ cup brown rice vinegar
¼ cup fresh-squeezed lime juice
¼ cup organic tamari
2 tablespoons honey
1 teaspoon sea salt
Pinch of cayenne pepper (optional)
6 tablespoons toasted sesame oil
4 tablespoons chopped fresh cilantro leaves
1 tablespoon minced shallot

1. Preheat the oven to 325 degrees.
2. Place the sesame seeds on a cookie sheet and toast for 10 minutes. Set aside to cool.
3. Place the garlic, ginger, vinegar, lime juice, tamari, honey, salt, and cayenne, if using, in the blender. Pulse to combine.
4. With the motor running, drizzle in the sesame oil. Once emulsified, stir in the shallot, cilantro, and sesame seeds. Set aside.

(Note: only ¾ cup of this dressing is needed for this quantity of salad; reserve the rest for another use.)

To make the salad:

¾ pound mesclun
1 cup celery, thinly sliced
    on the diagonal
3 scallions, trimmed and thinly
    sliced on the diagonal
1 cup sugar snap peas,
    julienned
2 oranges, peeled and
    cut into sections
1¼ pounds boneless
    skinless chicken breast,
    cooked and sliced
¾ cup sesame-ginger dressing

1. In a large bowl, mix lettuces
   with celery, scallions,
   snap peas and orange
   sections. Toss with half
   the dressing and divide
   among the plates.
2. Toss the chicken with
   the remaining dressing.
   Top each salad with 4
   ounces of chicken.

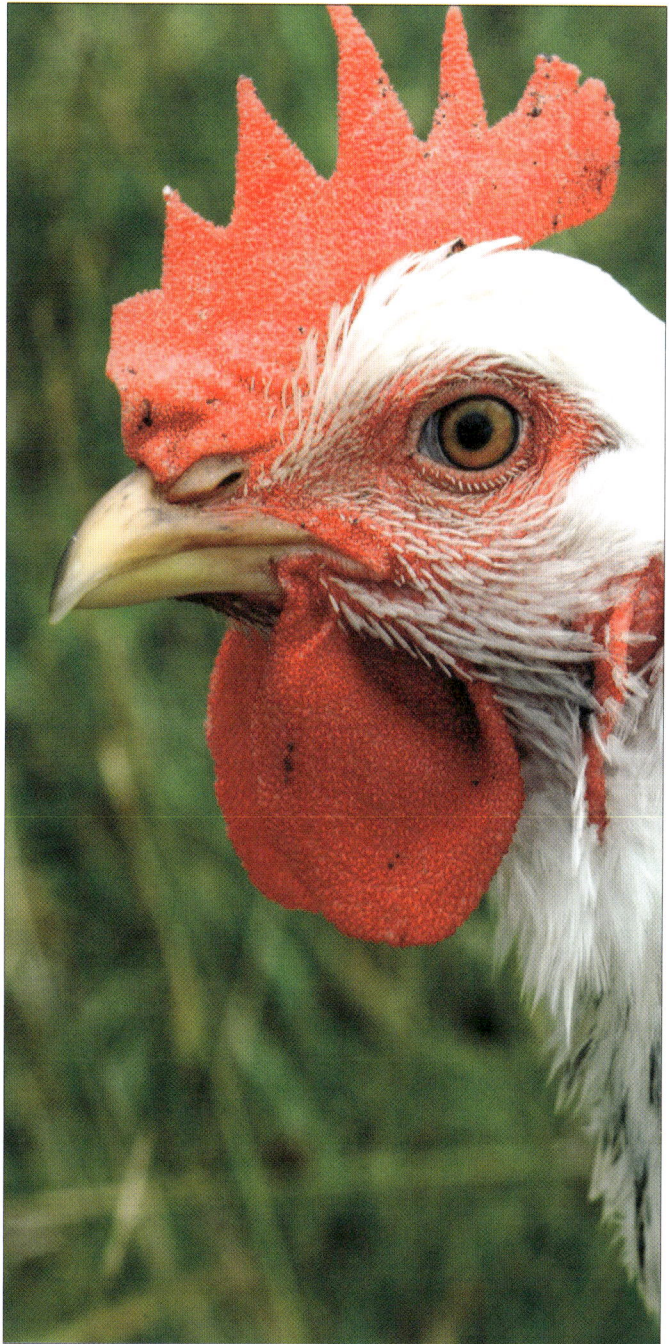

> "You have to
> win a battle
> a day."
> **–Patrick Dollard**

TheConversation Rethinking Healthy

DNA assistant chief Jennifer Franck (above right) and DNA executive chef Peggy Parten (left) discuss transitioning residents to a whole-foods, plant-based diet.

Jennifer Franck: *Sometimes we have kids coming in who only eat a few foods— like rice and chicken nuggets.*

Peggy Parten: *Transitioning them involves rethinking what healthy is. It doesn't have to be sprouts and tofu. Kids with autism can stress out at mealtimes, so you bring in familiar foods and it mitigates anxiety.*

JF: *It could be burgers, beef stew, or even chicken nuggets, just done in a healthier, DNA way.*

PP: *We start with a traditional method, by breading and sautéing organic chicken chunks. If they take to that we try it again with arrowroot, for a gluten-free version, if needed. We continue to pair familiar foods with new foods to encourage acceptance.*

JF: *They might not want to eat it today, but they usually will eventually. You have to keep trying new foods many times with kids.*

PP: *We have a non-pressure approach, which helps.*

JF: *We emphasize interacting with food, not just eating it. We want kids to touch and get to know the food without the pressure to eat it. Sometimes they paint with the food.*

PP: *Even getting a child to move a food off of their plate onto a "no thank you plate" can be an achievement.*

Chicken Liver Paté
with Marjoram and Apple | *DNA* ~ Makes about 3 cups

L iver, higher in micronutrients than kale, is the epitome of a nutrient-dense food—but it can be an acquired taste. To win over picky eaters, DNA chefs tend to use chicken livers, which have a much less pronounced flavor than beef liver. Smear the paté on a piece of baguette or a slice of apple.

1. In a sauté pan over medium heat, melt 6 ounces of butter. Add the bacon and sauté until the fat is translucent, about 3 minutes.
2. Add the onion and sauté until pale golden, about another 5 minutes. Add the garlic and stir for 1 minute.
3. Add chicken livers, apple and marjoram. Sauté until livers are just slightly pink inside and apple is soft, about 6 to 8 minutes.
4. Transfer the mixture to a food processor, then add the hard-boiled eggs, cognac or bourbon, and salt. Puree until smooth.
5. Transfer the mixture to a sieve and force it through the mesh into a mixing bowl. This will give the paté a silky texture.
6. Make sure the remaining 6 ounces of butter is softened. Return the paté to the food processor and add the softened butter. Season with freshly ground pepper.

12 ounces unsalted butter
4 ounces chopped bacon
1½ cups chopped onion
1 clove garlic, minced
12 ounces trimmed
    chicken livers
1 peeled and cored
    Granny Smith apple,
    cut into ⅓-inch dice
1 tablespoon
    chopped fresh
    marjoram
2 large hard-boiled eggs,
    peeled and
    quartered
2 tablespoons cognac
    or bourbon
1¼ teaspoons sea salt

Tables for All

Eating around a table with friends and family is a pleasure so basic it is easy to take for granted. But what happens when the people you are gathered with are in different-sized wheelchairs that don't fit under the standard dining room table?

Like many care facilities, The Center wrestled with wheelchair seating. There did not seem to be a way to keep diners together, given the disparate heights of wheelchairs, but president and CEO Patrick Dollard objected to the arrangement. "I didn't want these people in wheelchairs sitting in corners. I wanted them to have the experience of eating together with others," he says.

Thus began the effort to create an adjustable-height table that could accommodate diners of different sizes, shapes and ages as well as variations in chair size. Individual tables stacked on blocks to make them higher, or made shorter by cutting down the legs, were set next to the main table with other diners.

Over time The Center developed a design for a 30-inch "FlexTable" that could be lowered seven inches or raised six inches, depending on the needs of the student. "First one house wanted the table, then another, then one classroom, then another," recalls Peter Dollard, Patrick's brother, who oversees The Center's ergonomic design work.

"The table just took off."

Today the FlexTables are used throughout The Center, in classrooms, during therapy, and for dining in the residences and other locations across campus. They are made in two-station units that can be connected so that four, six and eight people with different needs can all dine or participate in other seated activities at the same time. "It's about ergonomics," says Peter Dollard. "People come in different sizes. So do wheelchairs. We call the FlexTable 'the table for all.'"

Sage, Parsley and Garlic Roasted Organic Chicken

Harold Moore ~ Serves 4

The executive chef of Harold's Meat + Three in New York City, DaVinci Master Chef Harold Moore is known for his simple but sophisticated food. "I think of my parents, who are straightforward and unpretentious," explains Moore, who prepared this roast chicken dish—using herbs from Thanksgiving Farm—at a seminar for The Center's residential cooks. It has become one of Chef Casella's favorite ways to make a bird at home.

1. Preheat the oven to 400 degrees.
2. In a small bowl, mix together the butter, parsley, chives, garlic and thyme.
3. Place the chicken in a large oven-proof sauté pan or roasting pan.
4. Using your fingers or a spoon, loosen the skin over the breast, taking care not to tear it.
5. Slip half the butter mixture between the skin and the flesh of each side of the breast. Now, using your hands outside the skin, smooth the butter over the entire breast.
6. Liberally season the cavity with salt, then tie the legs together with butcher's twine.
7. Season the outside of the bird with salt and freshly ground black pepper and place on the middle rack of the oven.
8. Roast for 1 hour or until a thermometer inserted into the thickest part of the thigh (without touching the bone) reads 165 degrees.
9. When the bird is cooked, transfer it to a platter to rest briefly.
10. Pouring off excess fat, return the pan to a burner over medium-high heat. Add the chicken stock, bring to a bubble and loosen the brown bits from the bottom with a wooden spoon.
11. Allow the liquid to reduce slightly while shaking the pan to emulsify the fat and the liquid. Taste and adjust the seasoning of the pan gravy.
12. Finish with a squeeze of lemon juice and the chopped herbs.
13. Carve the chicken and spoon gravy over each portion. Serve immediately.

¼ cup unsalted butter, softened

2 tablespoons minced Italian parsley leaves

1 tablespoon minced fresh chives

1 garlic clove, finely chopped

2 teaspoons minced fresh thyme leaves

3½-pound free-range chicken, wing tips removed

¼ cup low-sodium chicken stock

1 lemon, halved

1 tablespoon mixed chopped herbs, for garnish

Fine sea salt

Freshly ground black pepper

Chicken Adobo
with Tamari and Chives | *DNA* ~ Serves 4

A 3- to 4-pound chicken

½ cup organic tamari

1½ cups apple cider
  vinegar

9 bay leaves

1½ tablespoons whole
  black peppercorns

1 pound carrots, peeled
  and cut into ¼-inch dice

2 onions, chopped

2 green bell peppers,
  cored, seeded and
  cut into ½-inch dice

1½ heads garlic, peeled,
  cloves minced

1 tablespoon garlic powder

1 tablespoon onion powder

2 tablespoons olive oil

4 cups chicken stock
  (or water)

4 cups cooked white rice

1 bunch chives, chopped

The Center is a very multicultural place, with staff from around the world, and DNA menus reflect those influences. This Filipino chicken dish is well-loved by all.

1. Cut up chicken. Keep leg and thigh in one piece and cut breast in two halves. Save the rest for chicken stock. There should be 4 serving pieces.

2. In a large bowl, mix half the tamari (¼ cup), half the apple cider vinegar (¾ cup), bay leaves and peppercorns to make a marinade. Add chicken parts and refrigerate for 30 to 60 minutes. Turn the pieces every 15 minutes, making sure all have contact with the marinade. While the chicken marinates, prepare the carrots, onions, green peppers and garlic.

3. Remove the chicken from the marinade and pat dry. Mix the garlic and onion powders together and sprinkle evenly over the chicken.

4. Place the olive oil in a large braising pot and heat over medium-high heat until shimmering. Sauté the chicken in batches, turning the pieces halfway through, until they are nicely browned. Transfer pieces to a plate as they brown. Set aside.

5. Remove all but one tablespoon of fat from the pan and add the onions, peppers, and garlic. Sauté for 3 minutes, watching carefully—the garlic must not brown. Return the chicken to the pan along with the marinade, the remaining tamari and vinegar, and the stock or water.

6. Bring to a boil, reduce to a simmer and cook, covered, for 50 to 60 minutes. Add the carrots and continue cooking, covered, 25 to 30 minutes, until meat falls off the bone. Make sure the sauce remains at a slow simmer.

7. Remove bay leaves and peppercorns and discard. Pour the pan juices into a large measuring cup. The fat will rise to the top; spoon it off and discard. There should be about 4 cups of liquid. Remove chicken skin and bone before serving. For each portion, place one piece of chicken with accompanying vegetables over rice, moistening with ¼ cup of cooking liquid. Garnish each serving with fresh chives.

Chicken Curry with Coconut Milk
and Fresh Gingerroot | *DNA* ~ Serves 12

Chef Parten suggests serving this rich and flavorful chicken over steaming white basmati rice. A green vegetable on the side completes the meal.

1. Cut each chicken into 8 pieces—2 drumsticks, 2 thighs, 2 breast halves, 2 wings. Save the wings and backs to make stock. Remove skin from all pieces.
2. In a small bowl, mix together the salt, cumin, coriander, turmeric, cayenne, and black pepper. Sprinkle half this mixture on the chicken and allow to sit for at least 1 hour or overnight in the refrigerator. Reserve the remainder of the spice blend.
3. Place the garlic and ginger in the food processor with the water. Blend until fairly smooth.
4. Put the oil in a sauté pan over medium-high heat. When oil has begun to shimmer, add as many chicken pieces as the pan will easily hold in a single layer, working in batches if necessary. Brown lightly on both sides, then transfer pieces to a sheet pan.
5. Add the onion to the pan and sauté until medium-brown.
6. Add the garlic-ginger paste. Stir until all the water from the paste has evaporated. Add the remaining spices to the pan. Stir for about 20 seconds.
7. Add the chopped tomatoes. Turn the heat down to medium-low and cook for 3 to 4 minutes.
8. Add the yogurt a little at a time, incorporating each spoonful into the sauce before adding more.
9. Add the chicken pieces and any accumulated juices, as well as the chicken stock or water. Bring to a boil, then lower to a simmer. Cover and cook for 20 minutes.
10. Add the garam masala and coconut milk. Mix gently. Turn the heat up to medium-high and cook, stirring gently every now and then, until the sauce has reduced slightly and become fairly thick.

3 whole chickens, about
    4 pounds each
2 teaspoons salt
6 teaspoons ground cumin
1½ tablespoons ground
    coriander
1½ teaspoons ground
    turmeric
¾ teaspoon cayenne
¼ teaspoon freshly
    ground black pepper
18 peeled cloves garlic
2-inch piece of peeled fresh
    gingerroot, finely grated
1½ cups water
6 tablespoons extra-
    virgin olive oil
1½ cups chopped onion
1 generous cup whole
    peeled canned
    tomatoes, drained
    and chopped
¾ cup Greek low-fat yogurt
1½ cups homemade
    chicken stock or water
3 teaspoons garam masala
1 cup canned unsweetened
    coconut milk

CHAPTER FIVE

The Orchard

t is one of upstate New York's most cherished fall rituals: setting out with friends and family to pick apples at the local orchard. As the weather cools in September, thousands of fruit lovers fan out across the state to pitch in with the harvest of some 25 million bushels of Delicious, Empire and other favorite varieties. The air is crisp, the grass pale green and thinning. Row upon row of trees laden with golden and crimson apples stretch out in a swath of bounty. Happy pickers wander the corridors, sampling the autumn offering.

The scenario is no different at Thanksgiving Farm, where students, bundled in sweatshirts, caps and windbreakers, stroll with friends and teachers through the four and a half acres of trees in search of low-hanging fruit. Some walk, some sit in specially designed track wheelchairs, and all easily navigate the gentle terrain. It is a favorite time of year for the students, some of whom help mulch, prune and weed around a half-dozen types of apple trees as part of their farm chores. When the harvest comes they get to see—and taste—their hard work.

"We try to get as much of The Center crowd involved as possible," says Brett Budde, head herdsman, who also oversees the orchard. "Some of the resident houses will bake apple pie or make applesauce. [Director of Outdoor Education] Jim Cashen travels the campus with a cider press; kids drop in the fruit and watch as the mesh bag fills up with apple chips. It's the coolest thing."

The apple program has expanded rapidly over the past few years, after Thanksgiving Farm's previous orchard was severely damaged in a hailstorm. The farm team planted two parcels of replacements, quickly building to 600 apple trees. In the first year the harvest was 50 bushels; since then the yield has grown by leaps and bounds—in 2013 the farm produced 500 bushels. Soon there will be even more, as the Center has just planted a new orchard

Recipes

of 1,200 trees bearing the New York state fruit.

In addition to filling pies and making applesauce, the fruit goes into various baked goods, is dried to create snack rings, and is included in The Center's menu rotation. Fuji, Liberty, Ida Red and other varieties pair deliciously with the farm's honey and maple syrup. The apples are also part of a new initiative to make apple cider vinegar, a product with a long history of aiding a variety of health problems such as digestive disorders, joint pain and diabetes.

But most of all, the apples are a way for Center residents and staff to experience the wonder and bounty of nature. "The atmosphere the orchard brings about… there is something magical about it," says Jean-David Derreumaux, who oversees the biodynamic farming program.

Project Apple Cider Vinegar

When your orchards produce more apples than even a community of 2,000 people can eat, when you are looking for the healthiest possible ingredients to give that community, and when you are eager to try different ways of creating those ingredients, what do you do?

You try producing raw apple cider vinegar.

That was the thinking behind one of DNA's newest initiatives, making organic raw apple cider vinegar (ACV). A product that has generated much interest in the health community for potential benefits (aiding digestion and helping with blood sugar levels), ACV is easily and inexpensively made, and for The Center, offered a great way to use the apple crop and create another organic ingredient for DNA chefs.

Experimenting with ACV also dovetailed with the work The Center has been doing with natural fermentation as a way of boosting the levels of healthy bacteria in foods served on campus. Lacto-fermented pickles, gingered carrots and sauerkraut have become favorites at mealtime and it made both nutritional and ecological sense to add another naturally fermented food into The Center's diet.

Commercially produced ACV is created using pressed apples and yeast, but DNA opted for the wild catch fermentation process, where apple juice is placed in open barrels with no added yeast. Instead, staff stretches cheesecloth over the barrel opening to keep out the bugs, and the wild yeast and bacteria in the air and the skin of the apples kick-start the fermentation process.

ACV has been used in traditional cultures for centuries as a cure-all and science is taking a look at what treatments can be proven. The Center's small batches of ACV are as delicious as the apples they are made from, and that's what matters most.

"You can taste and smell our apples in it," says DNA chief Cesare Casella. "It's like a bite of fall."

Blueberry-Stuffed French Toast | *DNA* ~ Yield: 16 portions

"This French toast could also be used as a bread pudding for a lightly sweet dessert. At The Center we serve it at breakfast with Greek yogurt for added protein," says Executive Chef Peggy Parten. "Just a little drizzle of maple syrup and it is a perfect brunch." French toast needs a night to absorb its juices, so start this recipe the day before you plan to serve it.

1. Use the butter to grease a baking pan measuring about 10 by 12 by 4 inches.
2. Pour the orange juice into a saucepan. Bring it to a simmer and reduce to half the volume. Cool.
3. In a medium bowl, beat the reduced juice, eggs, orange zest, milk and salt until well-blended.
4. In a small bowl combine blueberries and sugar.
5. Arrange half the bread cubes in the baking pan. Dollop the cottage cheese on top, then evenly distribute the blueberries over the cheese. Top with the remaining bread cubes.
6. Pour the juice-egg mixture over the top and cover with a layer of parchment paper. Wrap the baking dish in aluminum foil and refrigerate, allowing the bread to absorb the liquid overnight.
7. Preheat the oven to 350 degrees. Remove the French toast from the refrigerator and bake for 1 hour. Remove the foil and bake uncovered for another 20 to 30 minutes. The center should be just barely set. Allow to cool slightly before cutting.
8. Sprinkle each serving with almonds and drizzle a little maple syrup on top. Serve with ½ cup Greek-style yogurt, if you like.

2 tablespoons butter
2 cups orange juice
12 large eggs
1¼ teaspoons fresh grated orange zest
1⅓ cups milk
⅛ teaspoon salt
3 cups fresh or frozen blueberries (thawed and drained if frozen)
1 tablespoon granulated sugar
4 quarts whole wheat bread in ½-inch cubes, loosely packed (about 2 pounds)
2 cups cottage cheese
½ cup sliced almonds
Maple syrup
Greek yogurt (optional)

Maple Syruping

*W*ith DNA's focus on local, seasonal and nutritional products, it was only a matter of time before Thanksgiving Farm began producing maple syrup. New York State is the second-largest producer of maple syrup in the nation, and maple syrup is the most nutritious of sweeteners, packed with manganese, riboflavin, zinc and other nutrients.

Every spring, families and students visit farms around the state to see how maple syrup is made, and when Jim Cashen, the director of outdoor education, first thought about producing syrup, he had in mind a nature lesson for residents. In 2009 he tapped a few trees and prepared the syrup on a stove in the Carriage House kitchen with the help of a DNA chef. The reception was enthusiastic, and the project quickly expanded. By 2014, residents were helping tap 250 trees. Next up? More trees, maple cream and maple sugar.

Maple-Pecan Baked Apples | *DNA* ~ Serves 4

This recipe combines two of Thanksgiving Farm's most-loved products—apples and maple syrup. Be sure to eat the skin, too: it contains more than half the fruit's fiber.

4 Braeburn, Fuji or other apple variety that holds up well during baking
½ cup pecans
¼ cup raisins
3 tablespoons shredded coconut
4 teaspoons maple syrup
¼ teaspoon lemon zest
⅛ teaspoon ground cinnamon
⅛ teaspoon nutmeg
4 tablespoons apricot jam or preserves
⅔ cup apple juice
4 teaspoons salted butter

1. Preheat oven to 375 degrees.
2. Core the apples. Using a small, sharp knife, peel the skin from the top third of each apple and cut a ¼-inch-deep line around the apple where peel and flesh meet. Cut a thin slice off the bottoms so apples don't tip over.
3. Place apples in a baking pan.
4. In a food processor finely chop the pecans, raisins and coconut. Transfer to a small bowl.
5. Mix in maple syrup, lemon zest, cinnamon and nutmeg.
6. Divide filling equally among apples, putting about 3 tablespoons in the hollow of each.
7. Spread 1 tablespoon preserves on top of each apple.
8. Combine apple juice and butter in a small saucepan. Stir over medium heat until butter melts. Pour into the baking dish with the apples. Cover loosely with foil.
9. Bake apples for 30 minutes. Remove foil, then bake until apples are tender, basting with juices every 10 minutes, about 35 minutes longer. Serve warm with pan juices.

Pear and Cranberry Cobbler | *DNA* ~ Yield: 16 servings

Thanksgiving Farm has only a handful of pear trees. One way everyone gets a taste is by making this cobbler. The sweetness of the pears is offset perfectly by the tartness of the cranberries (high in antioxidants) and the punch of ginger.

1. Preheat the oven to 325 degrees.
2. Prepare the filling. In a large skillet melt 2 tablespoons butter. Add the pears and sauté until they are slightly softened.
3. Remove pears from the heat and stir in cranberries, brown sugar, cornstarch, lemon juice, cinnamon and ginger.
4. Spoon the mixture into a 3-quart baking dish.
5. Prepare the biscuit topping: In a large bowl combine the flour, granulated sugar and baking powder. Stir in milk and eggs until just combined. Melt and fold in the remaining ½ cup butter.
6. Spoon the biscuit topping over the pear filling. Place the dish on a rimmed baking sheet and bake for 55 to 60 minutes, until the top is browned and the filling bubbly. Serve warm.

2 tablespoons plus ½ cup salted butter, divided
5 pounds pears, peeled, cored, cut into ½-inch chunks
2 cups fresh or frozen cranberries
⅔ cup dark brown sugar
6 tablespoons cornstarch
4 tablespoons lemon juice
4 teaspoons ground cinnamon
½ teaspoon ground ginger
2 cups all-purpose unbleached flour
½ cup granulated sugar
2 teaspoons baking powder
4 tablespoons whole milk
2 large eggs, lightly beaten

Thanksgiving Farm Best Apple Pie | *DNA*

After students help with picking the apples at Thanksgiving Farm each fall, residential chefs like to bake this apple pie as a treat.

For the crust:

1½ cups all-purpose unbleached flour

¾ teaspoon granulated sugar

⅛ teaspoon sea salt

9 tablespoons cold salted butter, cut into ½-inch cubes

1 tablespoon fresh-squeezed lemon juice

7 tablespoons ice water

1. Place the flour, sugar, and salt in the bowl of a stand mixer fitted with the paddle attachment. Mix for a second or two to blend the dry ingredients.
2. Add the cold butter, then run the mixer a few turns to coat butter pieces with the flour mixture. Turn off the mixer and remove the bowl.
3. Using your fingers, squeeze butter and flour into thin flakes of flour-coated butter. Return the bowl to the mixer stand.
4. Combine the lemon juice and ice water.
5. With the machine running at a low speed, sprinkle in the lemon water. Mix just long enough for the dough to barely pull together into a shaggy mass.
6. Divide the dough in half and pat each piece into a flattened disk. Wrap in plastic wrap and chill for about 30 minutes.
7. To roll out the dough, place a piece of plastic wrap on a cutting board and sprinkle lightly with flour. Place a disk of dough on the floured plastic.
8. Lightly flour the dough and cover with another piece of plastic wrap. Begin rolling from the center outward. Continue rolling evenly around the dough until you have a 12-inch circle. Settle dough into a 9-inch pie pan.
9. Roll out the second disk of dough in the same way. This will be the top crust.

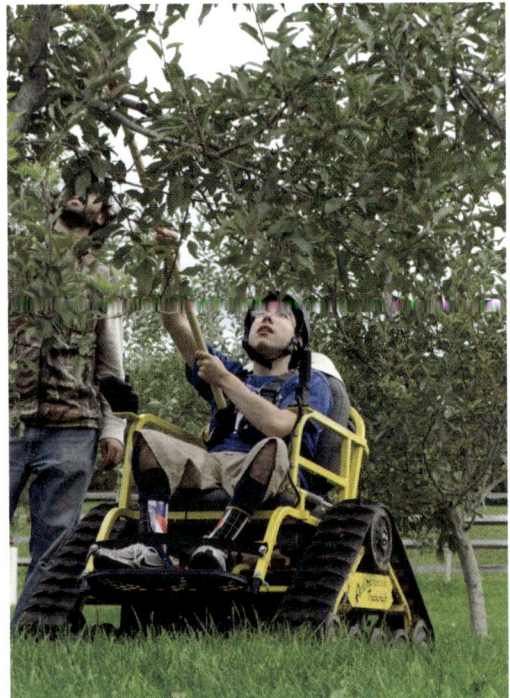

Apple picking time is a favorite with The Center's residents.

For the filling:

2¾ pounds apples (Braeburn, Fuji or similar), peeled, cored and cut into ¼-inch slices (yield: about 8 cups)
1 tablespoon fresh-squeezed lemon juice
¼ cup dark brown sugar, packed
¼ cup granulated sugar
¾ teaspoon ground cinnamon
¼ teaspoon nutmeg
¼ teaspoon sea salt
2 tablespoons salted butter
4 teaspoons cornstarch
1 egg yolk
1 tablespoon water

1. In a large bowl combine the apples, lemon juice, both types of sugar, cinnamon, nutmeg and salt; toss to mix. Allow apples to macerate at room temperature for at least 30 minutes but no longer than 3 hours.
2. Transfer apples and their juices to a colander set over a bowl to catch the liquid. The mixture will release at least 2 cups' worth.
3. Combine the liquid with the butter in a small nonstick saucepan. Bring to a boil and cook down to ⅓ cup, or until syrupy and lightly caramelized. Swirl the liquid occasionally as it cooks but do not stir.
4. Transfer the apples to a bowl and toss them with the cornstarch until all traces of it have disappeared.
5. Pour the syrup over the apples, tossing gently. (Do not be concerned if the liquid hardens on contact with the apples; it will liquefy during baking.)
6. Transfer the apple mixture to the pie shell. Moisten the border of the bottom crust by brushing it lightly with water, then place the top crust over the fruit. Tuck the overhang under the border of the bottom crust and press down all around the periphery to seal. Crimp the border using a fork or your fingers.
7. With a paring knife, make about 5 evenly spaced 2-inch slashes, starting about an inch from the center and radiating out.
8. Cover the pie loosely with plastic wrap and refrigerate for 1 hour to chill and relax the pastry. This will maintain flakiness and help keep the crust from shrinking.
9. Mix the egg yolk and water to make a wash. Apply the wash to the crust with a pastry brush.
10. Place a baking sheet wrapped in foil (to catch any overflow of juice from the pie) on the lowest rack position in the oven. Preheat to 425 degrees.
11. Set the pie directly on the foil-wrapped sheet and bake for 45 to 55 minutes or until the juices bubble up through the slashes. (Keep an eye on the crust as the pie bakes. If it is browning too quickly, cover lightly with aluminum foil.)
12. When the pie is ready, the apples should feel tender but not mushy when a small sharp knife is inserted through a slash.
13. Remove pie from oven and place it on a cooling rack. Allow to sit for at least 4 hours before cutting.
14. Serve warm or at room temperature.

Honey Bottling

Honey has a smell that we all know, but how to describe it? Warm, golden, a very particular kind of sweet, not sugary but like a field in summer. Breathe in deeply. It's December and you are in the honey bottling class at Thanksgiving Farm. The room is bright white, filled with light.

Two students and their teachers have already finished a lesson on bees and how honey is made, and now have come to the practical task at hand. One student fills the jars from a stainless steel vat and passes them to his classmate to close with screw-top lids. The tasks require hand-eye coordination, focus and social skills, and both young men are engaged and steady in their progress.

With the conclusion of class comes the reward. "Everyone gets a spoon at the end," says farm education systems coordinator Autumn Ackermann.

Apple-Pear-Date Compote | *DNA* ~ Yield: 4½ cups

This versatile spiced cooked fruit can be used in many ways. DNA chefs add it to oatmeal, or spoon it onto plain, tart yogurt to encourage eaters with a bit of a sweet tooth. The fruit releases just enough liquid while cooking to make the compote moist. "Heat diminishes the beneficial properties of honey, so we stir it in last," says Chef Parten.

6 pears, peeled, cored and cut into ½-inch dice
1½ tart green apples such as Granny Smith, peeled and cut into ½-inch dice
15 dates, pitted and diced
½ cinnamon stick
⅛ teaspoon ground cardamom
2¼ teaspoons vanilla extract
2 tablespoons honey

1. Combine all ingredients except vanilla extract and honey in a saucepan. Heat over medium until the fruit releases its moisture, then cover and simmer for 10 minutes or until fruit is tender (cook longer for a softer consistency).
2. Discard the cinnamon stick. Stir in vanilla and honey.

Creamy Blueberry Parfait | *DNA* ~ Serves 6

Thanksgiving Farm currently produces about 3,000 pounds of raw honey each year, most of which is used by the bakery. It is especially good in this parfait.

6½ cups rolled gluten-free oats
3 tablespoons sunflower seeds
3 tablespoons seedless raisins
1½ cups apple juice
¾ cup whole milk
3 cups frozen blueberries
4 tablespoons honey
3 cups plain yogurt
3 bananas, sliced ¼-inch thick

1. In a medium bowl, mix oats, sunflower seeds, raisins, apple juice and milk.
2. Cover and let sit in the refrigerator overnight.
3. The next morning, place the blueberries in a blender. Add the honey and puree.
4. Stir the oatmeal mixture well and spoon ½-cup portions into 6 bowls. Top each with ½ cup yogurt and sliced bananas and drizzle with pureed berries.

Pink Ginger Lemonade | *DNA* ~ Yield: 1½ quarts

"This drink is so pretty and refreshing!" says Chef Parten. "If you can't find currants, you can substitute cranberries."

1 cup freshly squeezed lemon juice
1 cup granulated sugar
Pinch of sea salt
3½ cups warm water
Large knob of fresh gingerroot, peeled
½ cup red currant base (see recipe)

1. Mix lemon juice, sugar, salt and water. Stir to dissolve sugar.
2. Place a fine strainer over a small cup. Using a microplane zester or a fine grater, grate the peeled ginger. Using your fingers, squeeze the grated ginger over the strainer to produce ginger juice. You will need a tablespoon of this liquid. Stir ginger juice into the lemonade and add ½ cup of the red currant base.
3. Serve over ice.

For the red currant base:

3 cups fresh red currants (or cranberries, fresh or frozen)
½ cup granulated sugar
1 tablespoon orange zest
½ cup orange juice
1 tablespoon Cointreau

1. Preheat oven to 350 degrees.
2. Place currants, stalks and all, in an ovenproof container. Add sugar, orange zest and orange juice. Mix. (Alternatively, you can combine these ingredients in a pot and simmer on the stove top.) Cover and bake for 45 minutes.
3. Cool slightly, then pass through a food mill.
4. Stir in Cointreau.

The Conversation
Going Step by Step

DNA assistant chief Jennifer Franck and DNA executive chef Peggy Parten discuss how Thanksgiving Farm helps shape The Center's nutritional program.

Peggy Parten: *The farming piece of the program is key. The farm and seasons guide our menu and how we meet the dietary needs of each person here.*

Jennifer Franck: *The diet we offer is whole and plant-based foods, which is therapeutic by nature. No matter who eats it, the diet is beneficial.*

PP: *It includes very few processed foods. We have some pasta and flour, but that's about it.*

JF: *Already walking through the door, that is a different approach than what 99 percent of people eat. And once you have the farm and whole foods, you're already shaping the menu. It is also having a different approach to eating. Studies show that up to 70 percent of children with autism had difficulty with feeding before they were a year old. We know there can be high stress around mealtime.*

PP: *Eaters often fall into two categories: hyper, where they are oversensitive to foods and just want bland things, or hypo, where they have an under-sensitive palate and want spicy hot or temperature hot.*

JF: *We have kids who won't tolerate a new food in the room. Eventually foods make it onto the table, then the plate. There are about 30-plus steps between a food being in the room and going happily into the mouth.*

CHAPTER SIX:

The Bakery

The term "breaking bread" is used to describe one of the most fundamental acts of companionship. To sit with a friend or loved one to share this basic foodstuff is at once elemental, a symbol of the need we all share, and complex, a reflection of the profound connection we have in food. Similarly, to bake bread is to provide others with the staff of life—what could be more gratifying? At The Center for Discovery, the bakery is at the heart of a system of caring that begins on the plate and ripples out in concentric circles of nurturing and compassion. The bread made here is not just a mainstay of the human diet, it is an artisanal expression of the dedication to quality that characterizes every aspect of The Center's work.

The baked goods are by turns delicate and light, dense and moist, flecked with rosemary and sea salt or delicately sweetened with honey. They come in every sort: country French, peasant dough and sourdough; Italian ciabatta and focaccia; honey whole wheat and honey oatmeal for sandwiches. Their textures, flavors and aromas are proof of the bread makers' skills and commitment to what baker Joseph Rodriguez calls "being present"—a philosophy of 360-degree involvement that spans ingredients, time, temperature and space. In all, the bakers produce between 400 and 500 loaves a week of bread that is 90 percent organic, as well as baked goods like cookies, muffins, scones, brownies and gluten-free treats.

And the bakers do not work alone. One group of adult residents slices, packages and delivers loaves to the residences. Another adult group helps run the 3D Baking Company, a program that produces desserts to celebrate birthdays and other special events on campus. They work with instructors, experimenting with new flavors and smells and textures. Measuring and scooping help teach the students math, stirring and shaping refine their motor skills, class interaction builds communication skills.

Recipes

The Hurleyville Market

In 2014, The Center opened the Hurleyville Market, a café and store in a former antique shop in Hurleyville, New York. In addition to being the town's first coffee bar, it is a showcase for DNA and other educational programs at The Center, as well as a place for local artisans to sell their wares. Like the planned hiking and biking trail, which will convert an old rail line into an interactive park for the general public, the Hurleyville Market creates a broader sense of community.

"It is a great cooperative outlet," says Dollard. "We can sell products from The Center and offer artisans a place to show their work."

The Market offers the same handcrafted wood-fired artisanal breads and rolls, cookies, scones, brownies and muffins that are served to the residents and staff at The Center, "edible works of art" made with organic flours that incorporate seasonal fruits, vegetables and herbs. Customers who want to eat in the shop, or plan to take their lunch with them, can enjoy a daily soup or sandwich selection made by DNA.

The shelves are stocked with ceramic pottery created in Center classes, as well as handbags, messenger bags, hand-dyed scarves and vases by Center residents and local artisans. There are specialty products available seasonally, such as honey, maple syrup, tea and herbs that those who live and work on the farm help produce. The market also carries comestibles from local artisans, including Aunt Neenie's, a gluten-free line of baked goods, and Sleeping Bear Woodworks, which makes one-of-a kind rolling pins, cutting boards and pepper mills.

Thanksgiving Farm Focaccia | *DNA* ~ Serves 4 to 6

Sourdough bread production has been a staple of The Center's bakery for a decade, and just recently the bakers have begun adding sourdough starter to other types of bread, like Italian focaccia, with great results. It is untraditional but delicious, says baker Rodriguez. "You add in a little and it helps enhance the bread's characteristics."

1. Combine the warm water, levain and 2 tablespoons plus 2 teaspoons olive oil in the bowl of a stand mixer fitted with a paddle or dough hook. Combine the dry ingredients in a separate bowl and stir to incorporate.
2. With the mixer at low speed, slowly add the dry ingredients to the bowl. Then switch speed to high and mix until dough looks fully incorporated and is pulling off the sides. If doing this step by hand, knead for about 5 minutes, or until dough looks fully incorporated. (It's fine if it seems a little wet and sticky at this point.) Then put dough into a bowl.
3. Cover the bowl with a clean damp cloth or plastic wrap. Let sit for about 2 hours, or until dough doubles in size.
4. Thoroughly grease a 17-by-12-inch sheet pan with olive oil.
5. Scrape the dough out of the bowl onto the oiled sheet pan. Pour a little olive oil over the top of the dough and smooth it over the surface with your fingers.
6. Begin to stretch and pull the dough to cover the sheet pan, then let it rest for a couple of minutes. Resume, spreading and pushing the dough down and outward with your fingertips, making sure it reaches all the edges and corners of the sheet pan and is evenly spread out.
7. Sprinkle the kosher salt, black pepper and rosemary over the dough. Let it rest on the sheet pan for about 30 minutes, or until rising dough is even with top of sheet pan.
8. Preheat oven to 420 degrees.
9. Place the sheet pan with the dough on the middle rack of the oven. After 15 minutes, rotate the pan to ensure even baking. Bake another 10 minutes or until the crust is golden brown. Lift the side of the focaccia with a fork to make sure the bottom is fully baked.
10. Let focaccia cool for about 30 minutes and remove from the sheet pan. Slice and serve.

2¼ cups lukewarm water
½ cup liquid levain (sourdough starter; this can be ordered online)
2 tablespoons plus 2 teaspoons extra-virgin olive oil; additional oil for greasing baking sheet
4½ cups organic unbleached all-purpose flour
2½ tablespoons organic whole-grain rye flour
2 teaspoons dried yeast
1 tablespoon sea salt

For topping:
4 pinches kosher salt
4 pinches cracked black pepper
4 pinches finely chopped fresh rosemary

Asparagus and
Roasted Red Bell Pepper Pizza | *DNA* ~ Makes 6 slices

" **P**izza is a familiar and loved food," says Executive Chef Peggy Parten. "That gives it an edge when we're trying to add vegetables to a picky eater's diet." In this version DNA incorporates asparagus and roasted red bell peppers for vibrant color and a fun design.

For the dough (*makes one 16-inch crust*):

¾ cup lukewarm water

2 teaspoons dry active yeast

¼ cup rye flour

1 tablespoon whole milk

1 ounce extra-virgin olive oil

½ teaspoon sea salt

1½ cups all-purpose unbleached flour

1 cup whole wheat flour

Semolina, for dusting

1. Whisk ¼ cup warm water (95 degrees) together with yeast and rye flour in a mixing bowl. Let stand in a warm place for 20 to 30 minutes or until yeast is foamy.

2. Place the mixture in the bowl of a stand mixer fitted with a paddle or dough hook and add the remaining ½ cup of water plus the milk, oil, salt and flour.

3. With the mixer at low speed, blend the ingredients. Continue, gradually increasing speed to medium-high, until dough is smooth and elastic.

4. Transfer dough to a lightly floured surface and finish kneading by hand for just a few turns. It will still be slightly sticky. Form into a ball and place in a large oiled bowl, turning to coat.

5. Cover dough with plastic wrap and leave in a warm location until doubled in size, 1½ hours. Punch down dough and allow to rise for another 40 minutes.

6. Shape into a ball; transfer to a floured baking sheet and refrigerate. (If you are not using the dough right away, you can chill it for up to three days.) Remove from refrigerator and let dough come to 60 degrees, just cool to the touch, before shaping into crust.

7. Preheat oven to 500 degrees.

8. Dust the work surface with a mixture of flour and semolina. Using the fingers of both hands and pressing outward, stretch dough into a disk, rotating it as you go, until you have a 16-inch circle. Bake for 10 minutes (for crispiest results, bake on a pizza stone). Remove from the oven.

For the marinara sauce:

Yield: 8 cups
This is a large batch of sauce. Freeze half to use later.

1½ tablespoons extra-virgin olive oil
¾ tablespoon minced garlic
Pinch crushed red pepper flakes
4 cups whole peeled canned tomatoes
4 cups tomato puree
1 teaspoon dried oregano
⅔ teaspoon herbes de Provence
2 teaspoons dried basil
⅔ teaspoon fresh-ground black pepper
2 teaspoons sea salt

1. Place the olive oil, garlic and crushed red pepper flakes in a large pot and heat over medium-low until garlic turns white. Do not allow it to brown.
2. Crush the tomatoes with your hands and add to the pot. Add the tomato puree, dried herbs, pepper and salt.
3. Bring the sauce to a simmer and cook for an hour, stirring frequently to prevent sticking.

To assemble the pizza:

1 cup marinara sauce
2 cups grated mozzarella cheese
1 pound trimmed asparagus
2 roasted red bell peppers, charred skin and
    seeds removed (or use prepared peppers)

1. Wash the asparagus and trim the tough bottom inch.
2. In a pot large enough to hold all the asparagus, bring generously salted water to a boil. Add asparagus and cook no longer than 6 minutes—it should still be bright green.
3. Drain asparagus and promptly immerse in ice-cold water to stop the cooking. When cool, drain and set aside.
4. Drain any liquid from peppers and cut into bite-size pieces.
5. Preheat oven to 450 degrees.
6. Spread the crust with the marinara sauce and sprinkle with the mozzarella. Artfully arrange the asparagus and peppers on top. Bake for 7 to 10 minutes, until the cheese is bubbling and just beginning to brown around the edges.

The Oven

At DNA, even the bread oven fits into The Center's vision of an interconnected world. About twelve feet in diameter and eight feet high, the wood-burning brick oven has a hearth that weighs almost a ton and can fit between 60 and 80 loaves at a time. Its walls, filled with reflective sand that serves as insulation, are close to ten inches thick. Wood used to fire the oven comes from The Center's land, so the appliance runs on renewable, sustainable energy.

But what is most remarkable about the oven, a gift from Paul Fleagane, is how it operates. There are no electrical or mechanical switches for turning it on or off. Instead, the oven does its job thanks to the intuition of two bakers. They adjust the temperature by adding more wood, stoking the flames or letting the embers burn down. The bakers are simply in tune with the oven. They know, for instance, how the temperature changes when loaves are added to the hearth; they know the effects of the day's humidity on their product; they know when to replenish the wood, and exactly how much to add. "It's about being present," says baker Joseph Rodriguez. "It's an organic experience."

Cheddar-Cornmeal Scones
With Cumin and Cayenne | *DNA* ~ Makes 12 scones

1½ cups all-purpose flour

1 cup cornmeal

2½ teaspoons baking
powder

2 teaspoons granulated
sugar

1 teaspoon salt

⅛ teaspoon cayenne
pepper

½ teaspoon ground cumin

6 tablespoons cold salted
butter, cut into pieces

2 cups grated cheddar
cheese

2 large eggs, lightly beaten

⅔ cup whole milk

For the egg wash:

2 egg whites

1 tablespoon water

The spices used here give a Southwestern kick. Serve the scones with eggs in the morning, with chili, or on their own as a snack.

1. Preheat oven to 425 degrees.
2. In a bowl, whisk together the flour, cornmeal, baking powder, sugar, salt, cayenne and cumin. Using your fingers and working quickly, blend in the butter until the mixture resembles coarse meal. Stir in half the cheddar.
3. In a small bowl, stir together the eggs and the milk. Add to the flour mixture, stirring with a fork until it just holds together.
4. Turn the dough out onto a lightly floured surface, knead it gently 3 to 4 times, and pat into a 6-inch round.
5. Using a sharp knife, cut the round into equal-sized wedges. Arrange about 2 inches apart on a lightly greased baking sheet and bake for 8 minutes.
6. While scones are baking, whisk together the egg whites and tablespoon of water.
7. Remove scones from oven.
8. Brush the tops lightly with the egg wash and sprinkle with the remaining cheddar.
9. Return scones to the oven for 8 to 10 minutes more, or until they are golden and cooked through.

Cinnamon and Raisin Polenta Squares with Maple Syrup | *DNA* ~ Serves 6

In Italy, polenta typically gets a savory seasonal treatment: as a creamy accompaniment to stewed rabbit in winter, for instance, or with a medley of mushrooms in summer. Here DNA turns the milled corn into a sweet treat, topped with raisins and maple syrup tapped from The Center's own trees. Even though the tapping program has grown in the past few years, the trees have a hard time keeping up with the demand of Center residents and employees, who can't get enough of the nutritious sap.

4 cups whole milk

2 cups water

1 teaspoon vanilla extract

2 teaspoons sea salt

6 teaspoons granulated sugar

2 cups coarse whole-grain polenta

½ teaspoon ground cinnamon

2 tablespoons salted butter

2 tablespoons sunflower oil

½ cup raisins

½ cup toasted walnut halves

1. In a medium-sized saucepan, combine the milk, water, vanilla, salt and 2 teaspoons of the sugar. Bring to a boil.
2. Sprinkle in the polenta and cook, stirring constantly until it begins to pull away from the pan, about 40 minutes.
3. Rinse a large baking sheet with cold water and shake dry. Mound the hot polenta in the center of the pan, then use a spatula dipped in hot water to spread it out evenly. Cover with parchment paper and refrigerate until set, about 45 minutes.
4. Cut polenta into 6 squares. Mix the remaining 4 teaspoons of sugar with the ½ teaspoon ground cinnamon. Sprinkle each polenta square with ½ teaspoon of the sugar mixture.
5. Heat the butter and oil in a nonstick pan over medium heat. Add the polenta slices, sugared side down, and fry about 4 minutes, until golden. Sprinkle the tops with sugar, flip, and cook for another 3 to 4 minutes.
6. If working in batches, keep the first batch warm in a 200-degree oven as you finish the rest. Meanwhile, heat the syrup and get the fruit ready.
7. Serve the warm polenta squares sprinkled with raisins and chopped walnuts. Top with maple syrup and/or fresh fruit.

The 3D Baking Company's Favorite Cupcakes | Makes 12 cupcakes

At the 3D Baking Company, residents prepare sweets to celebrate birthdays and other special days on The Center campus. Houses order cookies, cakes and these cupcakes, and participating residents take the orders through a special website and bake the desserts as well. In place of chemical dyes to color the cakes and frosting, the 3D bakers use special vegetable purees like beet and spinach.

For the beet puree:

3 medium beets

1. Preheat oven to 400 degrees.
2. Slice off any leaves from the beets and scrub clean. Wrap the wet beets individually in aluminum foil and place on a baking sheet.
3. Roast for about an hour, or until the beet is easily pierced with a toothpick.
4. Remove from the oven and let cool completely. (You may want to use disposable gloves, as the beets stain). Peel off the skins and discard. Chop the beets and place in a food processor. Puree finely and set aside.

For the cupcakes:

½ cup butter (¼ pound), softened to room temperature

1 cup sugar

2 teaspoons vanilla extract

2 eggs, at room temperature

1½ cups flour

½ teaspoon baking powder

¼ teaspoon salt

¼ cup cooked, cooled and pureed beet (follow Steps 1 through 4 above or puree canned beets)

1 teaspoon lemon juice

⅓ to ⅔ cup water

1. Preheat oven to 350 degrees.
2. In a bowl, beat butter and sugar together until fluffy.
3. Add vanilla and mix well.
4. Add eggs one at a time. Mix well.
5. In a separate bowl, sift together flour, baking powder and salt.
6. Slowly blend half the dry ingredients into the butter mixture.
7. Slowly stir in the second half.
8. Once dry and wet ingredients are thoroughly incorporated, mix in the beet puree and lemon juice.
9. Slowly add water, just to the point where the batter becomes smooth and honeylike.
10. Divide batter evenly among the paper-lined molds of a 12-cup muffin tin.
11. Bake for 15 minutes, or until tops of cupcakes are golden brown.
12. Cool completely, then frost with strawberry buttercream frosting.

For the strawberry buttercream frosting:

You will have a little extra strawberry puree left over. Spoon it over ice cream or stir into plain yogurt.

1 cup ripe strawberries
Honey, to taste
2 cups sifted confectioners' sugar
1 cup softened butter, at room temperature
1 teaspoon vanilla extract
1 to 2 tablespoons heavy whipping cream

1. Wash and stem the strawberries and place in a food processor. Puree, adding honey to desired sweetness. Set aside.
2. In the bowl of a mixer, cream the butter and sugar at low speed until light and fluffy.
3. Pour in the vanilla and whipping cream. Mix for 2 minutes.
4. Add 1½ tablespoons strawberry puree and mix until blended.
5. Add more cream if necessary to give frosting a good spreading consistency.

The 3D Baking Company

The 3D Baking Company is where residents get their glow on.

The name "3D" stands for Discovery, Delicious and Delightful. But it is much more. It is a baking program for residents that integrates cooking lessons and workplace learning. The program also produces the kind of delicious home-style sweets everyone wants to celebrate with—desserts made without chemical preservatives, food dyes, enriched flour or, if the resident's diet calls for it, without eggs, gluten or chocolate.

The program started in 2013 when a handful of teachers were trying to solve a problem: Families wanted to celebrate residents' birthdays and loved bringing in cakes and other sweets. The trouble was, many of the treats came from the grocery shelf and were loaded with refined sugar and dyes.

But what if a group of residents who liked to cook began making birthday cakes and cookies for fellow residents—cakes made with whole foods? Cakes and cookies without petrochemicals? Sweets baked with organic eggs and butter and flour? With frosted flowers and leaves made from icing tinted pink with beet juice or green with spinach?

It was the beginning of the 3D Baking Company, a way of leveraging the residents' natural interest in sweets into a better way of eating them.

Chocolate-Honey Carrot Cake | *DNA* ~ Yield: 6 to 8 portions

2½ ounces unsweetened
chocolate

Butter for greasing pie tin

1⅓ cups all-purpose
unbleached flour

¾ cup cocoa powder

1½ teaspoons baking powder

1½ teaspoons baking soda

½ teaspoon sea salt

¾ teaspoon ground
cinnamon

¼ teaspoon ground
cardamom

3 large eggs, beaten

1¼ cups honey

¾ cup sunflower oil

2 teaspoons vanilla extract

1 tablespoon orange zest

¾ cup plain yogurt

1½ cups grated carrots

"The flavor of the honey really comes through in this cake," says Chef Parten. "You don't need to top it with frosting, just a dusting of powdered sugar, if anything at all."

1. Preheat oven to 350 degrees.
2. Melt chocolate in a double boiler and set aside to cool. Butter and lightly flour a 9-inch cake pan.
3. Sift together the flour, cocoa powder, baking powder, baking soda, salt, cinnamon and cardamom.
4. In a separate bowl, beat the eggs. Add honey and beat until light. Beat in the oil, vanilla and orange zest. Add the cooled chocolate and stir well.
5. Add the yogurt and stir until just combined. Stir in carrots and pour into the prepared pan.
6. Bake for 25 to 30 minutes or until a toothpick inserted into the cake comes out clean.

Note: These can also be made as cupcakes; in that case, bake for 12 to 15 minutes at 350 degrees.

The Conversation In This Together

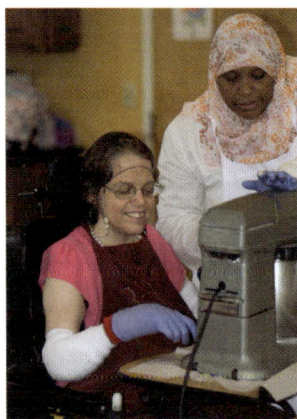

Patrick Dollard: *I really became aware of food security when my middle daughter was born. She was premature by ten weeks. They used to spray the nearby fields with dioxin and we only later learned how dangerous that was for the food supply.*

Cesare Casella: *Really? I was premature, too. I was born at 7 months, at home.*

PD: *I don't believe it.*

CC: *Yes. When I came out, the midwife said I was all nose. They took me to the hospital and put me in an incubator. They baptized me because they said this baby is going to die. I didn't speak until I was in first grade.*

PD: *This is where empathy comes from. We know these things first hand. We are in this together.*

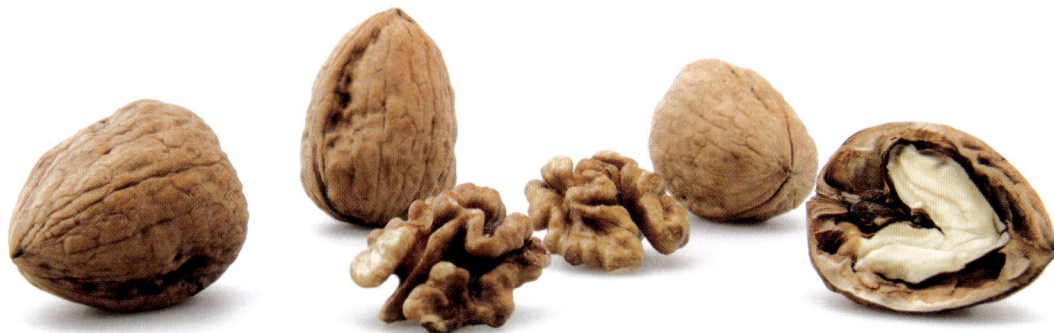

Greek Walnut Cake | *Maria Loi* ~ Yield: 12 portions

When DaVinci Master Chef Maria Loi decided to make this cake, called karidopita in her native Greece, she was inspired by the walnuts of up-state New York, but also by her own childhood. "I wanted to give a recipe of mine so the children at The Center could savor the same flavors I enjoyed as a kid," says Chef Loi. "I wanted the flavors of Greece to transport them to Greece."

1. Preheat oven to 350 degrees.
2. Combine water, sugar, orange rind and cinnamon stick. Bring to a boil and simmer for 4 minutes.
3. Remove from heat and stir in honey. Allow to cool to room temperature.
4. Combine the egg yolks and sugar in a mixing bowl. Beat until smooth and light in color.
5. In a separate bowl, beat the egg whites until stiff peaks form.
6. Combine the bread crumbs, walnuts, ground cinnamon and lemon zest.
7. Add 2 tablespoons of the dry ingredients and 1 tablespoon of the meringue to the yolk-sugar mixture and fold in carefully. Continue until all the dry ingredients and meringue have been incorporated into the yolk mixture.
8. Fold in the vanilla.
9. Brush a 9-inch round cake pan with olive oil and add the cake batter, spreading evenly. Bake for 40 to 45 minutes.
10. Remove from oven. Strain the orange peel and cinnamon stick out of the syrup and pour it over the cake. Once the cake has absorbed the syrup, top with 1 cup finely chopped walnuts.

For the syrup:

2 cups water

2 cups granulated sugar

Zest of 1 orange, in large strips

1 cinnamon stick

3 tablespoons honey

For the cake:

10 large eggs, separated

1 cup granulated sugar

1 cup plain bread crumbs

1 cup roughly chopped walnuts

½ teaspoon ground cinnamon

½ teaspoon fresh lemon zest

1 teaspoon vanilla extract

For the garnish:

1 cup finely chopped walnuts

The Dish of Hope

The Dish of Hope, a coaster-sized plate handmade by Center residents for tasting olive oil, is a combination of a good idea, good timing and good luck. A few years ago, The Center was trying to develop a pottery program in which residents could make dishes, mugs and other dinnerware. At the same time, Chef Casella, the chief of DNA, was looking for a prototype of an olive oil dish to sell at his restaurant in New York. Then The Center received a kiln as a gift and all the pieces fell into place, says Chris Kilgore, the recreation specialist who oversees the pottery program.

As DNA and recreational therapy departments collaborated to bring the idea to life, they decided to stamp the plates with the American Sign Language symbol for hope, which looks like a heart, and glaze them white so that anyone tasting olive oil can clearly see its color. Residents were introduced to the project during an olive-oil tasting that let them explore the aroma, consistency and flavor of wood-fired bread dipped in different oils ranging from fruity to peppery. For its debut, the Dish of Hope was given as a gift to guests at a Michael Ritchie Big Barn Event for a Sustainable Future in 2014. Today, residents who participate in the pottery program not only make the signature olive-oil tasting dishes, they produce plates, mugs, bowls, pitchers and vases, all of which are sold at the Hurleyville Market. "Everyone likes to do something different," says Kilgore. "Now we are trying to come up with a whole line of Hope pottery."

Gingersnap-Kabocha Cheesecake | *DNA* ~ Serves 16

Recently DNA has shifted from low-fat to full-fat dairy products to reflect its updated perspective on nutrition. "A little more full fat is OK," says Chef Parten. This cheesecake is high in fat, but also has the benefit of squash or pumpkin pulp to lighten it. It is a favorite for special events at The Center.

1. Preheat the oven to 325 degrees. Put ginger snaps and 3 tablespoons sugar in the bowl of a food processor and pulse to fine crumbs. Add melted butter. Press mixture into a greased 10-inch springform pan. Freeze for 15 minutes.
2. Beat cream cheese in a large mixing bowl until light and fluffy. Gradually add sugar. Beat in flour, vanilla, cinnamon, nutmeg, cardamom, allspice and salt.
3. Beat in eggs, one at a time, until smooth. Mix in squash puree or pumpkin.
4. Pour batter into crust in prepared pan. Bake on middle rack for 1½ hours, or until cake is firm around the edges yet still wiggles in the center.
5. While cake is baking, prepare the toppings. In a bowl combine the sour cream with the granulated or brown sugar and the Frangelico. Set aside.
6. Mix together dark brown sugar, flour, melted butter and walnuts. Set aside.
7. Ten minutes before the cake will be ready, remove from oven. Spread the top with the sour cream mixture. Then crumble on the candied walnuts. Return to oven and bake another 5 to 10 minutes.
8. Turn off oven and let the cake cool on the rack with the door slightly ajar for 2 to 3 hours. Remove from oven and cool completely on a wire cake rack.
9. Refrigerate, covered, for at least 2 hours or overnight.

For the crust:

24 ginger snaps
3 tablespoons granulated sugar
¼ cup melted butter

For the filling:

2 pounds cream cheese, at room temperature
1½ cups granulated sugar
⅓ cup all-purpose unbleached flour
2 teaspoons vanilla extract
1 teaspoon ground cinnamon
½ teaspoon nutmeg
¼ teaspoon ground cardamom
¼ teaspoon ground allspice
Pinch of salt
6 large eggs
2 cups kabocha squash, baked and pureed (or use canned pumpkin)

For the topping:

16 ounces sour cream
¼ cup granulated sugar or brown sugar
¼ cup Frangelico liqueur
½ cup dark brown sugar
2 tablespoons all-purpose unbleached flour
2 tablespoons melted butter
1 cup chopped walnuts

Dave Arnold mixes drinks

Cesare Casella and his DNA culinary team

Jennifer Franck speaks to guests

Patrick Dollard

Michael and Nelly Bly Arougheti

CHAPTER SEVEN

Michael Ritchie Big Barn Event for a Sustainable Future

The Michael Ritchie Big Barn Event, DNA's annual dinner for donors and supporters, is a case of a "thank you" paying off in unexpected and wonderful ways.

In 2010, to acknowledge the commitment and work of donors, parents and members of local government, The Center organized a special dinner, cooked by celebrity chefs at the Michael Ritchie Big Barn center. Mark Ladner, the chef of Del Posto, Anne Burrell of the Food Network, Kevin Garcia of 'Cesca and Accademia di Vino and Larry Finn of the Four Seasons, among others, were invited by Chef Cesare Casella to make a dish for the event. On the menu: Tuscan bread soup, farro made with Thanksgiving Farm honey and kabocha squash, chicken galantina, romanesco broccoli, braised brisket with autumn vegetables, and a pumpkin crème brûlée. The wine was as fine as the food, with bottles of Il Faggeto prosecco, Terlano Classico and other vintages provided by winemaker Lia Tolaini.

Instead of simply being celebrated as a one-off success, the Big Barn Event became a late-fall fundraising tradition that launched new programs with participating chefs. Many were so smitten they asked to get more involved in The Center's work. Chef Casella began bringing them up on a regular basis to hold classes for Center cooks on everything from knife skills to making stock and scaling recipes. That program was eventually formalized as the Cavaliere del Vinci, or DaVinci Master Chef program, which provides continuing-education training for Center

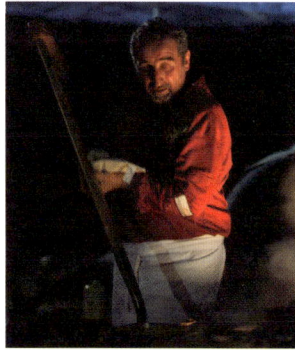

Clockwise from left: Chef Parten with Nils Noren; Chef Casella; Jessica Botta, Casella, Bill Telepan; Telepan, Johnny Iuzzini and Kevin Garcia; the kitchen at work

chefs by some of the best-known names in the restaurant industry.

"The event connected us to the New York restaurant world," says chief nutritionist Jennifer Franck. "It solidified our relationship with them and enriched our program." Today, 200 to 250 guests attend the annual dinner, and the roster of chefs who have cooked at the event or held master classes has expanded to include Bill Telepan of Telepan restaurant, Italian chef

Kevin Lewis, pastry chef Heather Carlucci, Greek chef Maria Loi, Carmen Quagliata of Union Square Cafe, Paul Denamiel of Le Rivage, Mexican chef Sue Torres, Pecko Zantilaveevan of the Four Seasons and Matt Abdoo of Del Posto.

The weekend of the event, many of the New York chefs arrive the night before and sit down to a special thank-you meal of their own. For the Big Barn dinner itself they are paired with as many as three or

four Center chefs, who help with the prepping and execution of the meal. Everything is made with seasonal Thanksgiving Farm ingredients and the evening is cozy, lit with candles and warmed with collaboration—"The coolest thing," says Franck. "We have world-renowned chefs helping each other on the line. We have Johnny Iuzzini asking Mark Ladner to crush something to finish the plate. All the chefs work together. You never get to see that."

The Big Barn

The Michael Ritchie Big Barn, with its autumn-red siding and distinctive stacked-on-a-hill silhouette, is an anchor of Stonewall Preserve Farm. Originally built as a cowshed, the Big Barn today is an educational center and a place for conferences, performances and special events. It is home to nine high-tech classrooms where groundbreaking research takes place along side schoolwork and it features a research garden where students learn cultivation techniques and grow a variety of heirloom herbs and vegetables. The Big Barn was built in honor of film director Michael Ritchie, whose stepson Billy Bly is a long time resident of The Center.

The basic structure was created artisanally, with mortise-and-tenon joints, and the flooring throughout is hemlock that was harvested from Center property, and milled at The Center as well. The building is cooled geothermally, with water provided by the Thanksgiving Farm irrigation system. It features 50 kilowatts of solar heating panels and has specially designed containers that catch rainwater that is later used for irrigation. As a model of universal design and sustainability, the Big Barn has the U.S. Green Building Council's highest possible environmental rating—platinum-level Leadership in Energy and Environmental Design (LEED).

ACKNOWLEDGMENTS

Now that we have collected the stories, recipes and work of The Center for Discovery and the Department of Nourishment Arts into *Feeding the Heart*, we would like to thank the extended family of supporters, friends and chefs who made the effort possible.

To start with, we thank the chefs and staff of The Department of Nourishment Arts who produce these dishes and transmit their enthusiasm and passion to The Center's residents and students. It is because of you we were able to create this book. To Peggy Parten, executive chef and culinary director, who worked with her team, led by Steve Granata and Theresa Preston, to review and test recipes, provide insight and guidance, and who injected humor into the recipe headnotes. Thank you to: Mike Acevedo, Patty Benevides, Nina Carraccia, Debra Castillo, Tom Drown, Noelle Dwyer, Mike Greene, Anthony Gonzalez, Dan Gonzalez, Yasmine Henriquez, Ann Hillriegel, Frankie Kutner, Frank Lark, Jacqueline Palmer, Dinytt Pla, Royal Porter, Theresa Preston, Tom Quackenbush, Jeanne Reiber, Joseph Rodriguez, Crystal Salgado, Eetmad Shehata, Elaine Smith, Della Vacquedano and Mark Wilcox. Additionally, thank you to Kevin Lewis and Miguel Monteros.

To the DaVinci Master Chefs who shared their recipes and vision with us: Franklin Becker, April Bloomfield, Heather Carlucci, Paul Denamiel, Michael Ferraro, Kevin Garcia, Will Hickox, Mark Ladner, Kevin Lewis, Maria Loi, Harold Moore, Nils Noren, Carmen Quagliata, Bill Telepan, Sue Torres and Pecko Zantilaveevan.

To art director Joe Dizney, who gave visual shape to our idea and made the pages beautiful.

To Jennifer Franck, whose editorial judgement and knowledge of food and nutrition influenced the contents at every stage.

To Richard Humleker, who helped shepherd the book from the very beginning, in addition to his more than full-time day job.

To copy editor and proofreader John Knecht, who met the not-so-simple task of keeping our copy clean.

To Steven Mosenson, general counsel, for his legal advice.

To Emily Pearson, whose enthusiasm, organization and understanding of The Center were key ingredients to *Feeding the Heart*.

To Jesse Wall, Dean McManus and Josephine Bono for capturing DNA, Thanksgiving Farm, staff, residents and our Center family in photographs. Additionally, thank you to Amy Hou and Sari Goodfriend.

To The Center staff who shared their time and stories with us: Autumn Ackermann, Brett Budde, Jim Cashen, John Conway, Jean-David Derreumaux, Matt Dingle, Peter Dollard, Tom Mead, Kerri Muzuruk, Petra Stephens, Joseph Rodriguez, Sam Rose, Mirna Solorzano, Deanna Winter and Greg York.

INDEX